THE
7 _most_
Powerful
SELLING
SECRETS
Soar Your Way to Success
With Integrity, Passion and Joy

By John Livesay

Edited by Ron Kraft

Advance Praise for
The 7 Most Powerful Selling Secrets...

"John Livesay's book identifies three critical ingredients to mastering the 'art of salesmanship' for today's business world—your voice, your energy, and your soul. John's unique insights into humanizing the sales experience makes this book a 'must-read' for newcomers, as well as seasoned vets. If you are looking for opportunities to update your tools of the trade and gain a competitive advantage in the sales arena, then look no further than this book!"
— Kevin Carroll, Creative Motivator to Nike® designers (aka The Katalyst), Nike®

"Take this journey with John Livesay and the roadmap of your career will be filled with nothing but green lights! As a journalist, his book has given me new ways to earn the trust of the people I interview, and found new tools that allow me to better trust myself and my instincts. *The 7 Most Powerful Selling Secrets* should be kept as a handy reference guide in every office, whether you are in real estate or reality TV."
— Robert P. Kovacik, Correspondent, *National Geographic* Channel

"John Livesay's vision and philosophy of using integrity and joy to connect to his clients translates into results that make him a consistent top performer at *W* magazine, as well as Fairchild publications. He was selected as the company's top salesperson of the year, out of the 700 Fairchild employees, in a company that publishes 15 titles. His book explains *The 7 Most Powerful Selling Secrets* in a way that everyone can use them."
— Alyce Alston, Vice President, Publisher of *W* magazine

"The emotional stamina and spiritual maturity to serve your customers is a vital ingredient to success in any profession, especially one as complex as sales. John Livesay has laid out a clear path of insightful how-to's that will take you through the roadblocks."

— Jeff Thull, CEO, Prime Resource Group and author of *Mastering the Complex Sale*

"John Livesay's book steps out on a path to maintaining one's self-respect, integrity and individuality during the selling process. This book is proof that you don't need to sell your soul to be successful in sales. It's about time the negative connotations that accompany the word 'sales' are rewritten."

— Michael Marriner and Nathan Gebhard, founders and authors of *Roadtrip Nation*

"Achieving success by finding a balance between the material world and the spiritual world takes great insight. In his book, *The 7 Most Powerful Selling Secrets*, John Livesay has discovered how to bring these two worlds together in a wonderful, intuitive and practical way."

— Char Margolis, author of *Questions from Earth, Answers from Heaven*

"John Livesay is one of those rare business executives who realizes that the things we all aspire to—influence, success, wealth—are directly proportional to the quality of our relationships. Having seen John in action, I've seen how he puts it to work in his career, and how integrity, passion and the other ingredients of successful relationships can produce amazing results."

— Jon Berry, Vice President, Senior Research Director, RoperASW, co-author of *The Influentials*

"At a time when there have been so many scandals in business and so much mistrust arising because of it, a book like John Livesay's is needed and welcomed in the business community."
— **David Palmer, Senior Vice President Marketing, Sony Pictures/Television®**

"At last! Spirituality and selling are finally combined to show how anyone can do business with heart. This book shows you how to integrate spiritual concepts with selling principles so you will become a better salesperson as well as a happier, more fulfilled human being. An inspiring book!"
— **Joe Vitale, author of the #1 best-seller *Spiritual Marketing***

"The most important secret in successful selling is integrity. Follow John Livesay's advice and you will enjoy selling every day in every way."
— **Kathy Aaronson, author and Chairman of *The Sales Athlete***

"WOW…here it is! *The 7 Most Powerful Selling Secrets* takes many of the trade secrets that selling professionals have learned over the decades and captures them in an easy-to-read and explosive style designed to captivate the mind and propel the body into success-inducing behaviors that can be sustained for enduring accomplishments. This blueprint for success details how to shine above others as a professional of integrity and valor, when it would appear society is bankrupt of both…this is a must-read!"
— **Jeffrey L. Magee, Ph.D., author of *The Sales Training Handbook* and publisher of *PERFORMANCE* magazine**

"It's no wonder that John Livesay's new book is called, *The 7 Most Powerful Selling Secrets: Soar Your Way to Success with Integrity, Passion and Joy,* because that's the way John lives his life, with integrity, passion and joy. John has proven that these secrets work and he offers them in a way that anyone can understand. Become the salesman you know you can be by using Mr. Livesay's *7 Most Powerful Selling Secrets.*"

— Dr. David J. Waker, Pastor, Los Angeles Church of Religious Science

By John Livesay

Edited by Ron Kraft

Richmond, VA

This is dedicated to the memory of my nephews
Jonathan and David.

The 7 Most Powerful Selling Secrets:
Soar Your Way to Success
with Integrity, Passion and Joy
© 2004, By John Livesay

Published by Palari Publishing
www.palaribooks.com

Permissions Department
Palari Publishing
PO Box 9288
Richmond, VA 23227-0288

Library of Congress-in-Publication Data
Livesay, John.
The 7 most powerful selling secrets : soar your way to success with integrity, passion and joy / by John Livesay ; edited by Ron Kraft.
    p. cm.
Includes index.
  ISBN 1-928662-04-8
1. Selling. 2. Success in business. I. Title: Seven most powerful selling secrets. II. Kraft, Ron. III. Title.

HF5438.25.L585 2004
658.85—dc22

Edited by Ron Kraft
Printed in the United State of America

Table of Contents

John Livesay is a child of the Abundance generation.
They are not a set demographic with an exact age, race
or regional context. They are a way of thinking, a psy-
chographic. To John, things are more valuable as they become
abundant. When one of his ideas starts to get used by a client,
the idea grows in value—it doesn't slip through his fingers.

In business he competes with players from the Scarcity
Mindset generation. They are everywhere. This generation sees
value when there is scarcity. High demand and low supply
equals higher prices and profits. Their world is ruled by supply
and demand. They see the pie of life as shrinking. "Keep it close
to your vest" is their prevailing wisdom.

Fear is the primary tool in the Scarcity Mindset, and Faith
is the dominant asset in the Abundance Mentality. This is an
age-old battle, but it lies at the heart of all of today's conflict,
both personal and professional.

In 1980, Alvin Toffler predicted the rise of people like
John when he wrote *The Third Wave*. Here's what he said:

> *"We are the final generation of an old civilization and the*
> *first generation of a new one, and that much of our personal*
> *confusion, anguish and disorientation can be traced directly*

to the conflict within us, and within our political institutions, between the dying Second Wave civilization and the emergent Third Wave civilization that is thundering in to take its place."

This book is a walk through John's mind. I advise you to wear good shoes. To take this walk and derive the book's true value, you need to subscribe to the Abundance Mentality. You'll need to believe that Customers are by their nature loyal and reciprocal. You'll see others' successes as something that is great—not something to envy or resent. You will have to view the pie of life as abundant; there is always enough to go around.

If you read this book with a Scarcity Mindset, you'll scratch your head wondering how John has reached his plateau of success. You'll see his generosity as foolish, risky and vulnerable. You'll question his ability to lead salespeople in a dog-eat-dog world. You will miss the subtle nuance of his relationship advice, distracted by the infinite trust that John bestows on his Customers to do him right.

The following book will take you on a journey that will enlighten you and change the way you think about your sales career. The first step, according to John, is a personal inventory of yourself and your feelings. This is important, so don't skip this difficult but rewarding step. The next five steps systematically walk you through the process of building your value, your brand and your unique proposition. You'll understand the roots of loyalty, the secret to competition and the difficulties that lie ahead. The final step is the one that resonates with me the most—give something back. Obviously, John has had the benefit of mentorship. Someone took the time to teach him values and principles, along with charms and tactics (probably in that order). This book is his way of passing on the knowledge, or as I like to say, Sharing the Love.

Sales is not a career, it is a symptom. You were born to convince, delight and keep Customers. It is not a game. It's a core competency combined with a conviction.

There are various levels of intelligence you need to reach for potential: intelligence, emotional intelligence and spiritual intelligence. This book seeks to offer all three.

Tim Sanders
Love is the Killer App: How To Win Business and Influence Friends
www.timsanders.com

Acknowledgements

My gratitude to my parents and sisters, Elizabeth and Barbara, for their support and love. My special thanks to my gifted editor, Ron Kraft, whose guidance, direction and insight always pushed me to try harder and do better. His contribution was so impactful and detailed that working with him on this book made the whole process soar. Also thanks, as well to Dena White for her tireless copyediting efforts. To my publisher, David Smitherman, at Palari for seeing the potential in this book. To Steve Rohr—my incredible publicist. To all my colleagues at *W* magazine, with a special thank you to Mary Berner, Patrick McCarthy and Alyce Alston. I am also grateful to Tim Sanders, Kevin Carroll, Jeff Magee, Char Margolis, David Palmer, Joe Vitale, Kathy Aaronson, Jeff Thull, Mike Marriner, Nathan Gebhard, Peggy Faracy-King, Max King, Stephanie Faracy, Richard Ayoub, Bradly Bessey, Jim Chabin, Dana LeVan, David Ault, Tim Casey, Dr. Mel Yoakum, Kristen Cooper, CJ Poust, Dr. David Walker, Dr. Brian Gold, Cooper Neal, Dennis Hammer, Elaine Gordon, Roger Davis, Francoise Gilot, David Haugland, Jim Rogers, Roy Huebner, Michael Moser, Dan Lipman, Ron Cowen, Lee Lessack, Dr. Bradley Frederick, Bruce Stevens, Alan Mercer, David Roach, Diane Silberstein, Joe Tremaine, BJ Von Netzer, Kramer Winslow, Rani Stoler, Jonathan Herbert, Arthur Johns, Jay Kerwin, Ken Best, John Nagler, Mary Ryan-Sigmond, Mecca

D'Amico-Dolio, James Mellon, Kevin Bailey, John Fry, Ron Fenley, Ray Davi, Kirk Gerou, Larry Ginsberg, Jon Berry, Dan Janal, Mark Williams, Janet Suber, Robert P. Kovacik, Donna Estes Antebi, Cheryl Woodcock, Devon Rothwell and Mark Spohn. Finally, a special thank you to all my clients who make this journey into selling one of joy and passion.

How to Succeed in Business (and in Life)

When I first started out in sales, despite having some good initial success, I used to fear that someone was going to tap me on the shoulder and say, "I'm sorry, there has been a mistake. You see, we know you're a fake. We know you aren't good enough. We know you don't really know what you are doing." Needless to say, my self-doubt created a lot of stress.

So I decided to read as many books on selling and attend as many selling seminars as I could to become more comfortable with my selling skills. As I became more informed, I became even more successful. However, I still felt there must be more to my career (and life) than just making my quota.

And there is. After selling in the computer and magazine advertising industries for over twenty years, I have learned to define success not only financially, but also by achieving a sense of inner peace about who I am and the contributions I make to others at work and at home.

By continuously taking sales training seminars and reading sales books such as *The One Minute Salesperson* by Spencer Johnson, I mastered the basics of selling. Concurrently, I also took classes in spiritual growth, and read books on spiritual awareness like *A Return to Love* by Marianne Williamson, *The Four Agreements* by Don Miguel Ruiz and *There is a Spiritual*

Solution for Every Problem by Dr. Wayne Dyer to name but a few. And from those books I learned an entirely different set of basics. By combining these studies, I have realized the importance of having my identity be larger than my job description. This realization has made such a huge difference in both my happiness and my success that now I want to share what I have learned with you. This book will show how to integrate spiritual concepts into selling principles that together will make you a better salesperson as well as happier, more fulfilled. As I said, it's worked for me. Once I started to integrate these spiritual concepts into my selling, I became more relaxed and happier. I also became more successful. In the last ten years, my income has tripled. This book will show you how you can use these very same concepts to achieve greater happiness and more success for yourself as well.

Perhaps some of you are thinking, *Well, I'm don't make my living from selling*. For you, I would still offer: All of us have to sell ourselves all the time. Whether or not we are selling a specific product or service, we still sell ourselves to get hired, have our ideas implemented and be promoted. When we sell ourselves, we are selling our integrity, our value and our ability to do what we say we will do. The people who can sell their concepts and their value most successfully get paid the most.

If you are a student, you need to sell yourself to gain admission to the college of your choice. If you are interviewing for a job, you need to convince the person hiring to pick you. If you're a real estate agent, you need to convince buyers that you are the right person to find their dream home. If you're a talent agent, you need to sell the services of the actors, writers and directors that you represent. If you're a publicist, you need to convince the media to give press coverage for your clients. If you work for a car dealership, you need to convince people to buy from you instead of a competitor, regardless of the price. If you sell computers or office equipment, you need to convince the purchasing staff to buy your brand or to buy a brand widely available...from *you*.

How you feel about yourself when you are selling directly impacts the results you achieve. If you are trapped in self-defeating and negative perceptions about who you are as a seller and why you are selling, it will be a struggle to be successful. Many salespeople, both seasoned and newcomers, realize they have an emptiness or lack of fulfillment in their lives. They may also feel that they are unable to reach that next level of success in their careers and may not be able to identify the reason. If you would like to learn new ways to gain trust and respect from buyers so you can be more successful and feel proud of what you do and how you do it, this book is for you!

How was Michael Dell, of Dell Computers®, able to go from college dropout to founder and CEO of one of the most successful technology success stories? How was Benjamin Zander able to go from abandoning the cello (when his hands became too painful to play) to being the founding conductor of the Boston Philharmonic? How was Howard Schultz able to go from growing up in federally subsidized housing in New

York to being the chairman of Starbucks Coffee®? They all had an inner belief in their abilities; and that belief allowed them to overcome obstacles by the seemingly simple act of following their inner passion and thereby finding a path to happiness and success. (Read more about them in the terrific book *Roadtrip Nation* by Michael Marriner and Nathan Gebhard.)

How would you feel if you could learn how to sell yourself like they were able to? What if you could learn *The 7 Most Powerful Selling Secrets* that would set you apart in anything you sell whether it is a product, a talent, a service or just yourself? What if you could learn to do all of this while also making other people feel more appreciated, uplifted and even inspired? This book will show you how to achieve these positive results and more.

By reading this book, you will learn to:

- Enjoy the sales experience as a way to express your creativity, individuality and spirituality.
- Eliminate fears of failure or rejection.
- Reframe negative perceptions you may have about the sales process requiring you to be pushy or aggressive.
- Create success by having a clear understanding of how you can make a positive difference in your world.

Beyond you and your personal world, the questions of how we interact in the workplace and what values we bring to the table reverberate everywhere in corporate America.

Scandals at Enron, WorldCom, Imclone Systems and other large companies make it seem like many corporations could use a little spiritual healing themselves.

This may be because the traditional business mindset frames all professional interactions in terms of doing battle for customers and market share, much like armies at war. In the '90s, Creative Artists Agency co-founder Michael Ovitz was quoted as saying he was going to "send his foot soldiers" to confront a well-known writer who was threatening to leave the agency. It was widely known that Ovitz had his staff read *The Art of War* by Sun Tzu. In the book it says, "All warfare is based on deception." The implication is to think of the buyer, the boss or the competition as the enemy and thus deception becomes the key to winning. While this may be a formula for a certain type of success, I have also found it to be an often toxic recipe for loneliness, self-hate and ultimately unhappiness. By reading this book, you will find out how you can be just as successful as one of Ovitz's foot soldiers and still sleep at night.

In the old paradigm of selling, the seller is commonly thought of as pushy and aggressive, or unreliable, without heart, believing only that the end justifies the means. He's like Willy Loman in *Death of a Salesman* or the character Jack Lemon played in *Glengarry Glen Ross* — desperate, pathetic, needy and dependent on others for approval and money. They are thought of as the type of people who'd sell their best friends down a river to make a quota.

This book is designed to show how you can change your perspective and see that honesty with buyers builds integrity and trust, and that honesty—with yourself and others—is a truly powerful thing. You will discover that being honest creates an environment of mutual respect and genuine reward. When you don't need to think of the competition as the enemy in order to be motivated, you can find your motivation in a far more powerful place—one of helping buyers succeed. Being nice will no longer be thought of as being weak.

Instead, your power will come from the knowledge that your identity is something that transcends the trappings that surround you. Nothing—whether it is a job, your car, your home, your boss or your income—defines who you are. I believe your identity in fact precedes anything you have or achieve. From that centered, connected place, you begin to learn that any actions you take to sell yourself or your ideas are not going to change your self-worth. Rather, they will give you balance and strength, much like standing on two feet instead of one. This integrated approach to defining who you are achieves two things:

- Gives you new tools for success.
- Gives you a new level of satisfaction about yourself and what you do.

This book will empower you by helping you to depend on the spirit within for confidence and self-worth. It will also give insight into landing a sales job and keeping your boss happy as well as obtaining new clients and keeping them happy. (Often sellers just focus on the buyer and shortchange their boss. More on this later.)

This spirit-based approach allows you to come from a place of "How can I be of service and help you meet your needs?" versus "What bargain with the devil will I have to make to close this deal?!" The results from this new approach can be transformational. For over twenty years in selling, I have used these spiritual principles with my clients and prospects with great results. Once you are coming from a place of calm—a rock-solid centeredness—you will know who you are and because of that knowledge, buyers will want to give you business. They sense that they can trust you.

In the first chapter, you will learn the first of *The 7 Most Powerful Selling Secrets*. This first secret will give you the ability to shift from a sense of desperate negativity to a far more positive place. You will learn how to hear other opinions of you or what you are selling without it affecting your confidence, and you will learn how to attract success! Each of the following chapters will reveal another of the proven techniques on how to attract success and attain your highest goals.

Is it really that easy? Seven steps and, *voila*, success? Well, yes and no. This book is a place to start, but at its end will you have arrived at the end of your journey? No. Your whole life is a journey. But *The 7 Most Powerful Selling Secrets* can and will make a powerful, tangible difference in your success and in your happiness with whatever successes you achieve.

Chapter 1
Creating Your Reality

"There is nothing either good or bad,
but thinking makes it so."
—Shakespeare

magine what it is like to be one particular movie star—handsome, happily married and rich. Your career starts out with success in the theatre and then progresses to the big screen where you get some small but noteworthy parts. After a nationwide search, you're cast to play a pop culture icon, beloved by millions. The movie is such a hit that several sequels are planned. In between sequels you land other film roles and take the opportunity to do more theatre, working with actors you'd only dreamed possible, like Katharine Hepburn. Beyond your career, you enjoy life and are extremely athletic. With your millions, you finally have the resources to indulge all your wishes for adventure in its many forms—cars, boats and horses. Then, in one second, a horseback riding accident paralyzes you from the neck down.

This actor is, of course, Christopher Reeve, and the movie that changed his career, *Superman*. What, to me, is so remarkable about his story is what he decided to do with his life after the accident. To go from playing Superman, a superhero with extraordinary physical capabilities, to someone who can't walk, eat or even breathe without assistance seems perhaps one of the biggest changes that a person could face. According to stories, despite the depression that Christopher Reeve has experienced, he has somehow managed to find the inner resources to believe that he will walk again. Perhaps, just as noteworthy, Reeve then made a monumental decision: to use his fame and personal story to raise money for a cure that would benefit the tens of thousands of others who are also unable to walk due to spinal injuries and defects.

I remember vividly when he made his first public appearance at an awards show, while hooked up to a ventilator, and received a standing ovation from his colleagues in the TV and movie industries. And since that singular moment, he has gone on to direct TV movies and raise millions for research. What gives Christopher Reeve the power to find meaning in his life despite the obvious changes to the life he once knew? Is there a connection between helping others and finding meaning in life? Does finding meaning in life bring happiness and success? The answer is yes!

Secret #1

Your thoughts create your reality.

Here's how the process works:

    —Your thoughts create your beliefs

    —Your beliefs create your actions

    —Your actions become your habits

    —Your habits become your character

    —Your character becomes your reality

Here is an example of this process. Let's assume you have this thought, "I am an honest person." When you find yourself in a situation where you have the choice to either act honestly or not, you follow your beliefs about yourself and do the right thing. You do these types of honest actions long enough, and they become second nature—your habit, if you will. After a period of time, this habit of being honest becomes one of your character traits embodying not only how you define yourself, but how others do as well.

A character trait can be measured by how you behave when no one is watching. For example, if you think you can steal something and no one would ever know, but you don't steal, that is a manifestation of the character trait of honesty. When your thoughts become fully integrated into who you are, they become your new reality. You are honest with yourself and honest with other people. Taking this even one step further, how you treat the world is how the world treats you. For instance, if you lose your wallet or purse, you believe that someone will turn it in because in your reality people are honest with you.

In sales, when you are honest with your clients, you give them a fair rate. Over time you begin to get referrals because you're viewed as someone who is a straight-shooter; someone who understands that in the best deals both sides walk away from the table with smiles on their faces. Clients may also buy from you, even when you don't have the best rates, because they know you treat them with honesty and respect.

In order to communicate your integrity, I have learned that the thoughts or words you say to yourself (what I call *self-talk*) are even more important than what you say to other people. After all, isn't the person with whom most of us have the majority of our daily dialogue ourselves? Is that conversation kind, patient and loving? Or is it impatient, angry and unforgiving? Do you express more negative thoughts than positive ones to yourself and about yourself? Do you believe that what you think about will come true? What would it take for you to shift the number of negative thoughts you have so that they are outnumbered by positive thoughts? Here are some common things people say to themselves. See which ones sound familiar to you...

Excuses

Negative	Positive
It just won't work	The things that need to work out will work out
I don't have enough time	I have plenty of time to think, plan and do
I'm always late	I have enough time to get where I need to be
I can't seem to get organized	Taking the time to get organized is just as important as anything else I do
Today just isn't my day	There are good things even on bad days
That really makes me mad	Getting mad is OK, getting over it is better
Another blue Monday	Monday is a great day for a fresh start
I don't have the energy I used to	I have the energy to do the important things
I never have enough money	Money is not the only definition of prosperity
Why even try?	All my efforts are rewarded
That's impossible	Nothing is impossible

Self-Doubt and Rejection

Negative	Positive
You can't trust anyone anymore	People trust me and I trust them
Nothing ever goes right for me	Things will turn out for the best
I don't have any talent	I am as talented as I need to be
I'm just not creative	Creativity flows through me all the time
I don't have the patience for that	I remain calm and centered
I'm too shy	People welcome me when I express myself
I don't have a chance	There are unlimited opportunities for me
I've never been any good at that	I can choose to learn anything
Someone always beats me to it	I only compete with myself
I never know what to say	When I'm myself, the right words will come to me

Now let's look at *self-talk* from a sales-specific point of view.

Negative	Positive
I'm just not a salesperson	People want to buy from me and they value my expertise
I can't take rejection	I never take rejection personally—I view "no" as just meaning "no for now, not forever"
This territory has no potential	Sales come from sources expected and unexpected
That buyer hates all salespeople	I always respect the buyer and therefore the buyer always respects me
There is too much competition	I am unique and what I have to offer has value

Using these *self-talk* sales examples are a great way to give yourself renewed confidence in your sales ability. Confidence comes from remembering that your identity as a spiritual being is independent of any one person's opinion and that you deserve success. When you come from the perspective that success is abundant, you realize there is more than enough for everyone.

In my own personal experience, the most amazing results have come from using the phrase "Sales come to me from sources expected and unexpected." An example of this involves Lucky Brand® jeans—a company that had spent little ad money in two years. I kept in touch with them anyway, updating them with the occasional note and phone call. One day, out of the blue, they called and said, "We now have a budget and want to work with you again." While I didn't stay in touch with the expectation I'd see any immediate business from them, I didn't give up on the idea that they might come back into the marketplace. I certainly didn't put them on my list of potential clients for the year. It was a great feeling to get the call that they had money to spend and that I was one of the first calls they made when they were ready to spend it. I didn't forget about them, and they didn't forget about me.

By being open to receiving business from accounts that you have focused on, and also willing to accept "guilt-free" sales from unexpected sources, you don't block the abundance that surrounds all of us. Since your thoughts create your reality, if you think you don't deserve a sale unless you worked really hard for it, then that will be true for you. By believing the universe is unlimited, you can take your career to the next step and accept that you don't have to know all the details of why good things come to you when they do. All you have to do is accept the fact that they will!

So, what should you do if you have a negative thought? Will all of your negative thoughts come true? How can you erase the effect of all these negative thoughts? I think that's a little like asking: Does one unhealthy meal really make you fatter? Does one wrong turn when driving mean you are lost forever? Does one sleepless night mean you will never sleep again? The answer is that it is the sum total of your thoughts that gives you your experience. One thought alone does not make you a success or a failure.

Giving yourself permission to have the occasional negative thought allows you to let go of the mistaken idea that you have to be perfect all the time in order to feel good about yourself or to be successful. Just keep thinking the type of thoughts that match your desired outcome so that 51% of your total is positive. Then you can keep working towards the ultimate goal of 100% positivity from there. When you find yourself thinking a negative thought, simply say "Next!" to yourself and replace it with what you do want. I have seen again and again that the spiritual universe responds to your thoughts in this moment.

Another way to visualize what I am talking about is to think of these thoughts as if you were shouting into a valley. The echo you get back is only what you just shouted out. This applies to what goes on inside your head just like it applies to the laws of nature. Each echo is fresh every moment and is not dependent on what you shouted five minutes ago or five years ago. You get back what you put out. Are you willing to begin the process to start a new echo? Give it a try. You have everything to gain and really nothing to lose.

Now, let's get started with changing those little voices inside your head.

Write down the three most common negative things you say to yourself and try to think of a positive alternative. Feel free to use any of the ones I described or write your own if none of these are right for you.

Negative

1._____

_____

2._____

_____

3._____

_____

Positive

1. _____

   _____

2. _____

   _____

3. _____

   _____

By focusing on just three each week, you will quickly discover how many times you think or say negative things and also have a tangible number to work on. The key to making a change for the better, however, is to say or write down the positive alternatives when you find yourself thinking or saying something negative. This is the first step to being in control of your thoughts, which will then start to change your beliefs. These new, positive beliefs will start to become your actions and then develop naturally into positive habits. The sum total of these habits is what shapes your character and gives you the power to control your experiences and create the reality you desire and deserve.

How long are you willing to keep thinking the thoughts that will make your dream a reality? Would you keep thinking something was possible for over four years, even if no one else had ever achieved it? What would you do if you got hurt trying?

Your instinct might be to say, "No, I wouldn't last that long, and I certainly wouldn't want to get hurt in the process." But take a look at the Wright brothers. They did all of that and more. In 1896, Wilbur Wright became interested in flying while reading about a glider pilot. This inspired him and his brother, Orville, to test their first glider in 1900—it was a complete failure. In fact, Wilbur broke his arm during the flight. They kept trying and by 1903, they kept their first plane in the air for 12 seconds, covering 120 feet. Wilbur was literally running alongside the plane as Orville flew it! It wasn't until 1904 that they made their historic flight. Do you have the same belief in the power of your thoughts? Do you give yourself permission to dream? Do you value all your successes, even if they only last 12 seconds? You should. Look what it did for the legacy of Wilbur and Orville.

Sales State of Mind

Let's look at how your thoughts create what I call the *Four States of Mind in Sales.* These different states of mind either work for you or against you in your efforts to create your own ability to fly much like it did for the Wright brothers. These thoughts, or states of mind, can change from day to day or moment to moment. The choice is yours to shift up to a higher state at any time. By using this awareness of where your thoughts are in the flight pattern, you will be able to achieve what I believe is the ultimate goal for every person selling anything, something I call *soaring above the radar.*

Four Sales States of Mind

1. *Not Selling:* This is like a plane being grounded—you don't make sales calls, you call in sick, etc.

2. *Just Selling:* The plane is on autopilot. You go through the motions of making sales calls. You give up easily when objections arise.

3. *Selling Without an Integrity Compass:* You demonstrate effort here, but without taking any risks or thinking outside the box. This is like the seller being the pilot and the buyer in

coach class with no input on any specifics of the flight. You only ask for the order once.

4. *Soaring Above the Radar:* The seller and the buyer are co-pilots. You ask for the sale at the right time and in different ways. You find out all the needs and objections, and you go the extra mile to be a partner with your buyer. You take risks by proposing things no one has ever offered before. You trust the process and honor all involved. The universe is navigating your course, and you trust that everything is happening in the right way and in the right time.

Soaring above the radar means going beyond the rote, mundane ways of selling, such as giving the same old presentation you've given a hundred times before. If you bore yourself, you're sure to bore the potential buyer. Once you learn how to connect with someone (your buyer or your boss) on a spiritual level, you will feel a renewed sense of exhilaration from your work and realize that this kind of satisfaction is really the ultimate destination. Now when you are soaring, you can recognize it by the feeling that you and the buyer are actually having fun. The process feels light and full of joy. You are having an adventure, and both sides are expressing their creativity.

Remember that you control your own destiny. By the simple act of consciously choosing your state of mind, you can influence and even control your own future. That feeling of empowerment is nothing less than exhilarating. Since your thoughts ultimately create your experience, affirmations are a great way to make sure your *self-talk* is putting you in the right *Sales State of Mind*. One powerful way to implement this selling secret into your own life (and one that has worked the miracle of shifting my own perceptions) is to say your positive affirmations to yourself as a way to start your day—particularly before a big meeting.

Remember Secret #1: Your thoughts create your reality.

So, now are you ready to give your thoughts their own personal preflight safety check? Can you see yourself and the buyer in the co-pilot seats sitting side by side? Are you ready to *soar above the radar*? You are if you think you are.

Quick Summary of Your Sales Flight Plan:

Secret 1

Your thoughts create your reality.

Your thoughts create your beliefs, which create your actions, which create your habits, which create your character.

Sales come to you from sources expected and unexpected.

Would you like to learn how to get along with all types of personalities? Would you like to increase the odds of having rapport from the moment you meet someone? Would you like to learn how to develop a connection that gives buyers a feeling of mutual trust and respect when dealing with you? Chapter 2 will show you the valuable secret that you will find useful and powerful in every arena of your life.

Chapter 2
Building Dynamic Relationships

"If in our daily life we can smile...not only we,
but everyone else, will profit from it.
—Thich Nhat Hanh

Building Dynamic Relationships

At his mayoral inauguration, his wife and son stood by his side. His election was the highlight of a long political career. Throughout his terms, he made controversial decisions about issues like art censorship and popular decisions like cleaning up the city. He was generally well-liked and respected. His political stock was high enough that he was seriously considering a run for the Senate. Then everything fell apart. The affair he had been having became tabloid fodder, which caused him to lose public support. That, combined with the fact that he was diagnosed with prostate cancer, caused him to abandon his plans for the Senate. Fearing that his political career was over, he moved out of the mayor's mansion. He still had the responsibility of finishing out his term, even though the rest of his term was looking as if it were to be the textbook definition of lame duck.

Then the unthinkable happened. Terrorists attacked New York City's World Trade Center, killing thousands. The President of the United States was put in temporary seclusion and the eyes of the entire country fell on Mayor Rudy Giuliani for guidance and reassurance. During the hours and days after the attacks, his impotent political status seemed to vanish. His visibility increased, not only in New York, but also worldwide, and his renewed confidence established trust and rapport across all socio-economic boundaries—from firefighters to heads of state. The compassion he showed set a new standard for government leadership and won him fans, even among those who had previously opposed him.

One of the most healing contributions he made was simply attending many of the funerals for New York police and firefighters, who died in the line of duty. By his very presence, he made the families of those who lost loved ones feel that their sacrifices were being very publicly acknowledged.

How easy is it for *you* to show compassion to others in times of great stress? At what point do differences and past mistakes dissolve, allowing you to focus on what you have in common with others? Do you ever feel like giving up on your career when you have one or more rejections or failures?

Through the simple act of compassion, Rudolph Giuliani was able to build a connection to many people across a broad social and political spectrum. His expressions of compassion also gave him a renewed sense of purpose and catapulted his stature to the national and international levels. This is the core basis of:

Secret #2

Compassion creates rapport.

Merriam-Webster's Collegiate Dictionary defines <u>compassion</u> as the "deep awareness of the suffering of another, coupled with the wish to relieve it." How often have you seen people in a job they hate? How often have you seen someone physically suffering from job stress? How often have you seen someone afraid they'll lose their job if they make one wrong decision? When you start to see the buyer as having these types of issues, and you come from a genuine desire to help them by first understanding and then acknowledging where they are, you begin to create rapport on a deeper, spiritual level.

In *Merriam-Webster's*, you also find a definition of <u>rapport</u> as "sympathetic compatibility—a relationship of mutual trust or emotional affinity." Can you see the connection between the definition of compassion and rapport? Do you see how rapport is much more involved and important than just being nice in the first few moments of meeting someone? Can you imagine how much better your experience and sales results could be with a deeper level of rapport?

Many times people talk about having rapport with someone from the first moment they meet. How does this happen? It's not about having your shoes shined or having a snappy opening line. People actually gain an impression of you through all of their senses. And in my experience, what they are scanning for is whether or not they are being judged. As a successful salesperson you will need to assess who your buyer is in order to speak to them in their own language. There is a simple rule to help establish you as a compassionate human being and build that rapport—keep your identity focused on being a source of love, and try to see the love in everyone you meet. If you do that one thing, rapport will come easily.

Some of you may be wondering, "Why even bother with this approach to building business relationships?" The answer is simple. People tend to buy ideas and products from people with whom they feel an emotional connection. An important aspect of establishing yourself as a trusted partner can be achieved by allowing people to feel safe. We naturally gravitate towards those who make us feel safe. People want to buy from those they trust to treat them fairly.

So, beyond being a source of non-judgmental love, how do we build rapport? One of the best ways is to let go of the desire to try to control others. Trust that the best results will happen, and then just relax. One way to exude trust is to trust yourself to come from a place of integrity. We can only get back what we give out. And we can only give out what we already possess. A simple way of explaining this idea might be to realize that you couldn't give someone a cookie if you don't have any cookies to give. So it logically follows that you can't give love if you don't have love yourself. And you can't get others to trust you until you trust yourself.

Our ability to be compassionate is rooted in the fact that no matter what side of the table we find ourselves on, at some point in time we have been on the other side. Having been there before gives us valuable insight into why certain actions lead to certain reactions. Each of us has experienced being the seller and the buyer, the employee and the boss, the tyrant and the victim. By putting yourself in the other person's shoes, you see them as an individual trying to do the best they can, instead of as an adversary. Centering yourself and operating from a place of understanding and compassion, you can identify what role the buyer is assuming. For example, when a buyer asks you for the best price, you can easily remember an instance when you were the buyer in a parallel situation and can understand their motivation for asking. Once you do that, it becomes easy to have the conversation about price without it being an adversarial situation.

Just as it is important for a doctor to remember what it is like to be a patient or a teacher to remember what it is like to be a student, it is important for a salesperson to remember what it is like to be a buyer. One way to do this is to remember a specific purchase you made that was significant to you, such as your car or home. Remembering the anxiety you felt when buying something that cost more than you had ever spent before will give you the compassion you need to ultimately close the deal when your buyer is having a hard time saying yes.

We can step outside of a specific problem or situation and rise above it by asking ourselves, "How can I see this in a different way?" or "Will this be important next week, next month or next year?" Taking yourself out of the specific moment and trying to give the experience a greater context allows you to transcend feeling stressed and lets you focus on what really matters. You will be amazed at what finding inner peace will do for both your happiness and success.

Rapport building is an important first step that should never be skipped and should continue throughout the entire sales process. One of the most common mistakes I have seen is that salespeople ignore this step and move right into their sales presentation.

Salespeople often spend too much time socializing (which is not the same as rapport building) and thereby fail to uncover the buyer's true needs or all of their potential objections to buying. Often the client will allow this to happen—it is not their job to lead the sales call, it's yours. People don't want to be controlled, but they *do* want to be in the hands of someone who knows what they are doing. The feeling you want to create with the client is that there is a competent, concerned person (you, the seller) flying the plane (with them—the buyer—right beside you of course). If you succeed at making them feel safe in your plane, they will know where the plane is going and that the seller knows the best route to get there. When the seller and buyer are co-pilots, the rapport flows easily.

These types of rapport-building tools just described, such as compassion and trust, are of a spiritual nature. However, to best succeed in sales and in life, you also need to marry the spiritual to the practical and consider the types of personalities you will encounter, how to recognize each and how to best work with all of them. There are three main types of personalities and each has a preferred way of developing rapport. Let's look at each one in detail:

I. The "Feeling" Person

Think of Katie Couric, the co-host of the *Today* show. To me (and millions of other Americans) she represents the "Feeling" type of personality. People of all ages respond to her warmth and humor. She is able to project a huge amount of empathy and concern about everyday people as well as her celebrity guests.

One great way to recognize the "Feeling" person is that they will often express their thoughts in terms of a comfort level with an idea or deal.

The best ways to create rapport with this type of personality are:

Use humor. These personalities love to laugh and be around people who make them laugh. The best way to make them laugh is to tell a self-depreciating story. Here's an example from my life: Shortly after I joined a local gym, I was riding on a stationary bike next to a friend. I leaned over to whisper something to him. After I was finished, I leaned too far the other way and fell right off the bike! The manager came over to see if I was all right, and all I could say was, "I bet I'm the first guy ever to fall off one of these bikes going nowhere." We have all been in a situation where we are trying to be cool, but end up looking like the fool. When you share a story where you were embarrassed and show you don't take yourself so seriously, it helps build a human connection.

Show the person, not just the deal, respect. "Feeling" types want to know you care as much about them, as a person, as you do about their business. One way to show your compassion with a "Feeling" person is by taking a sincere interest in their family. If they have family photographs displayed, make an appropriate comment. It's not a new tip, but if done with sincerity, it can be effective.

Extend an invitation to take their family to an upcoming event. For example, I was able to arrange a ride on a blimp with one of my advertisers. One of the clients in the blimp happened to live near the blimp base and had told his wife and kids to be outside in their yard in case they could see the blimp in the sky. The pilot offered to fly directly over his house and as low as possible. When the client saw his wife and kids in the backyard waving, he was ecstatic. We all went out to dinner afterwards and realized we had bonded over an experience none of us would ever forget.

II. The "Information" Person

Think of Bill Gates, founder of Microsoft, when you encounter this type of personality. Numbers and data are the key criteria for how they make their decisions. For this type of person, a decision can be made when you demonstrate how it all adds up.

You can recognize this type of personality because they

will always be peppering you with requests for more details and the numbers behind the numbers. Visually, you can often identify the "Information" type of person by noting that they rarely have clutter in their office and are usually very punctual.

The best ways to create rapport with this type of personality is:

Show them you are organized and have done your homework to prepare for the meeting. Never wing it!

Start your meeting by providing them with a timeframe for just how long the meeting will last.

Impress them by providing research data on their industry and competitors that they might not otherwise be able to access.

Once, I made the mistake of talking to an "Information" personality in "Feeling" terms. When I asked her if the offer I presented felt good, she grew upset, "I don't make decisions based on my feelings! The numbers have to add up. That is how I make a smart decision." Even seasoned salespeople like me can hit a wrong note when we're not in tune with who the client is!

III. The "Big Picture" Person

Think of Jeff Bezos, CEO and founder of Amazon.com. He is often described in the business press as the ultimate long-term thinker. His belief that nothing is impossible, or too big to make happen, is a key criteria for how he makes his decisions and defines him as a "Big Picture" person.

People like Bezos tend to see a project in terms of the grand scheme, and you can practically see their eyes glaze over once the conversation gets into the details. In my experience, they also tend to like to quote other "Big Picture" thinkers like Winston Churchill or consumer trend analyst Faith Popcorn. A good visual cue into this type of personality is that they will often have pictures of themselves with politicians or celebrities. Along with the pictures, they may also have the latest books on cultural or business trends proudly displayed on their bookshelf.

The best way to develop rapport with this type of personality is:

Speak in visual terms and explain how your proposed idea might fit into some future trend.

Compliment them by making sure you mention how their company is contributing to that new vision.

Follow up the meeting with a thoughtful gift, such as a book that speaks to their specific interest in trends or a recent biography of another "Big Picture" thinker.

Here is an example of my experience with this type of personality: I was in a meeting with the owners of Lucky Brand Jeans® at the time when they first started exploring the idea of advertising in magazines. (Remember them from Chapter 1? This meeting laid the groundwork for that sale from sources unexpected.) They were not interested in a presentation of dry demographic data about the age and income of our readers. So I followed their lead and talked about what was important to them. They wanted to associate their brand with the history of rock and roll. The part of the meeting that excited them was the brainstorming session where we discussed that having a legendary rock band perform at their trade show would be just the right way to make an impact. This is a completely different type of meeting than the one you will have with a "Feeling" or "Information" person. The challenge is to keep up and shift into "Big Picture" mode yourself!

Now that I've introduced the three main types of personalities, here is a summary of some of the best ways to develop and maintain rapport with any of them:

Have compassion for the people you are interacting with so they know you recognize their needs and feelings—see them as more than just a buyer. This is a key method of developing trust.

Reduce your personal anxiety by not worrying about whether or not the client likes you. Accept yourself and you won't be seeking acceptance from others in an inappropriate environment—the office. Remember that any anxiety you feel, the buyer will feel, too. People rarely want to buy when they are not relaxed.

Remember to be a co-pilot with your buyer. Adapt to their particular personality style—"Feeling," "Information" or "Big Picture." Mix your compassion with the practical reality of what is important to the buyer.

If you let selling come from a place of spiritual integrity, you then trust the rapport process enough to listen with an open heart. Doing so eliminates your need to seek approval from the buyer and, instead, lets you focus on their needs. You can then relax and let your true spirit come through. When buyers feel relaxed and feel you are being "real," they feel the connection and want to buy from you. Or, as Dr. Seuss once put it so wisely, "Be who you are and say what you feel because the people who mind don't matter and the people who matter don't mind."

Here is an affirmation for creating rapport through compassion. Say this to yourself before an important phone call or meeting, and watch as you and the buyer soar above the radar together.

AFFIRMATION

"I am now a co-pilot with my buyers. My compassion allows others to see me as I see myself, as a trustworthy person."

Quick Summary of Your Sales Flight Plan:

Secret 1

Your thoughts create your reality.

Your thoughts create your beliefs, which create your actions, which create your habits, which create your character.

Sales come to you from sources expected and unexpected.

Secret 2

Compassion creates rapport.

Recognize and react to personality types: Feeling, Information, Big Picture.

Be a co-pilot with your buyers.

What if you could find out how to take rapport to the next level and gain valuable information about the buyer's decision-making process? How would you like to be more confident and comfortable getting buyers to share their buying criteria with you? Can you imagine the excitement of being included in developing the buyer's criteria? How many more sales do you think you'd be able to land if you had access to this insider information to make your presentations soar? Chapter 3 will show you how to do this and more!

Chapter 3
Insight + Passion =
Presentations with Impact

"It is our choices that show what we truly are,
far more than our abilities."
— JK Rowling, *Harry Potter*
and the Chamber of Secrets

H ow can you gain insight into a customer's buying criteria even before giving your sales presentation? How can you know what the buyer is thinking? Is there a way for you to help the buyer define the elements they will use in their decision-making process? The answer is yes, if you show the buyer how they will benefit from sharing this information.

Merriam-Webster defines <u>insight</u> as: "The act of perceiving in an intuitive manner; the power of acute observation, deduction and penetration." Here are four simple but effective ways to give you insight into the buyer and put you on the inside track.

Benefit 1: Save the buyer time.

Assure the buyer of your commitment to them by outlining your strategy to maximize combined efforts. Statements like, "In order for me to make the best use of your time, I'd like to ask you a few questions about your decision-making process. Then I will know what relevant information to give you so you can make the right decision for your needs," let buyers know that you have carefully mapped out a plan that is flexible enough to meet their needs, and efficient enough to be practical.

Benefit 2: Make the buyer's job easier.

Earlier in the book, I emphasized the need for going beyond the rote questions that every salesperson asks and instead adding an emotional or spiritual component to promote relationship building. To start the journey down this path, pose questions like, "What is the best and worst part of your job?"

The first time you ask a question like this you may feel a little off the beaten path, but you will find it can uncover needs that lurk below the surface.

Here is how it worked for me: A media buyer once told me that the best part of his job was the thrill of getting the best price. The problem is, if I only have this information, the whole focus is on price—and in my mind that's never a formula for successful selling unless you're Wal-Mart®. Then I asked him about the worst part of his job, and he said that it was frustrating to have no system for tracking image ads in order to see if they were actually effectively increasing store traffic. (Here is a need that may not have come to the surface without asking this slightly "blue sky" question.) Buoyed by this new information, I developed a marketing program that targeted our magazine's readers. By offering a gift from the magazine when readers made a purchase of the item featured in the ad, we increased their sales by 10% for the month. The media buyer was thrilled that he had a way to prove actual sales resulted from his advertising and subsequently, his focus on price decreased.

Benefit 3: Make your buyer look good to the boss or stockholders.

Taking the emotional and spiritual relationship building to the next level requires asking questions like, "What is the number one thing that will make your boss happy?" Often the answer will be fairly predictable, such as delivering results on time and as promised. Still, I encourage you to ask and listen very carefully to the answer.

Getting to the point where your connection to the buyer is based on a collaboration focused on finding ways to make them look good may seem like a minor shift in approach, but it is one that will prove to have major results. If you can move from just being another salesperson to someone who is going to make the buyer look good to their boss, their stockholders or their clients, you have indeed started down the path of establishing a spiritual connection with the goal of becoming a valued partner.

Benefit 4: Make the sales process fun for everyone.

To take the relationship to the final level of connection,

try asking questions like, "What gives you joy?" If someone is not able to answer this question, either because no one has ever asked or they have never asked themselves, you can offer an example from your own experience to spark their imagination. Here is a story I have shared with buyers to show how I find joy in my job.

For me, one of the pleasurable aspects of working in magazines is the monthly arrival of each new issue. The happiness and excitement I feel when I see how months of work have come together is like the indescribable childhood joy of opening presents on my birthday. Seeing where the ads are positioned and what they look like enhances the experience. When I hold in my hand the tangible effort of so many creative people—from the compelling cover and feature stories crafted by the editorial team to the unique advertising vehicles and programs dreamt up by my talented advertising colleagues—the sense of fulfillment and pride transforms the arrival of each new issue into something joyous.

Another wonderful aspect of my job relates to my personal passion for photography. Since I collect photography, buy books about photography and enjoy taking pictures myself, seeing art-quality photography in the magazine's fashion spreads makes selling the ads easy and fun. If you can combine what you love to do away from work with what your work encompasses, you will almost naturally come to the sales process from a place of joy.

Understanding what gives your buyer joy is a key aspect

to making the sales process fun for you and the buyer. So many times people think that anything work related is, by definition, not going to be fun or joyful. Is taking the buyer to lunch at their favorite restaurant to celebrate the sale a way to bring them joy? Is there a way to show the buyer how a brainstorming session with you can tap into unknown levels of creativity and unearth new ideas to improve their business? Can you really ask the buyer questions such as, "Are we having fun yet?" to keep the process light and positive? Well, yes, and you should!

Just by keeping your awareness of joy as a *possibility* during your daily life, you will find spontaneous ways to introduce it into the selling process. Remember that your thoughts create your beliefs. So be sure you are thinking thoughts like, "Both the buyer and I can have fun *and* be productive at the same time." Many people talk about how doing something to help others succeed attracts success to you. Take this one step further: Do something for others to enjoy, and you will receive joy in return!

What this all adds up to is...

Secret #3

Show you care and buyers will share.

So now you have tools to find out what is important to the buyer. Without this information, you're trying to design a flight plan without really knowing where you are trying to go.

With this information, however, you are now ready to give a sales presentation that is custom made to meet the buyer's key criteria and thereby greatly increases your chances of connecting with the buyer and making the sale. Let's look at how to add passion to the insight you have gained.

Passion

A great way to be successful in sales is to focus on how you sell. A champion golfer focuses on their golf swing, a world-class singer practices scales before a performance, a renowned doctor continues to study the latest techniques and an award-winning actor rehearses their lines before a performance. You need the same level of focus, practice and passion to take your selling to the level of soaring above the radar.

For selling purposes, passion can be defined (*Merriam-Webster*, once again), as "boundless enthusiasm." You will need this passion to break through the clutter of the other presentations buyers will hear. You want the buyer to not only share information with you as discussed above, but also to share in your passion for what you are selling.

Before we get to the secrets of infusing passion into the sales process, let's take a step back and review the ideal structure of a sales presentation. It is:

• Sell yourself

• Sell the company

• Sell your product

With this foundation, your presentation will always be on solid ground. When you sell yourself, you are not selling the details of your background or your image, but rather your identity and your compassion. When you sell your company, whether you own the company or not, you are selling its integrity. After your compassion and the company's integrity are established, you've laid the groundwork to sell your specific product or idea. Your personal passion is what makes the sale happen.

As an example of how passion makes all the difference in the world, let's start with the basics and look at what you need to do to get hired for a job—in sales or elsewhere. Landing a new gig is probably the one time where everybody has to sell themselves, no matter what their chosen career. Therefore, in the job interview, you must be passionate about wanting the job you're seeking and not just desperate to get hired. You have to remember that you are the product, and you have to show the people hiring you that your passion for that product (your drive and self-esteem) will fit seamlessly into the company's culture. So, what can you do to make yourself stand out? How can you keep cool and confidant during what can be an intensely nerve-wracking process?

As I said above, to effectively sell your assets, you must first be sold on yourself. You have to believe in your heart that you deserve the job and, moreover, that you deserve the best that life has to offer—prosperity, good friends, loving relationships and work that brings you joy.

If we all deserve a job we enjoy, why does one person get chosen over another? From my experience, what differentiates the successful job candidate from the unsuccessful one is an awareness and belief in your own infinite abilities. From this emotional place of strength, you can prepare yourself for an interview, knowing you are just as good as other candidates *and* as the person doing the hiring. A simple, helpful trick for putting the interview process in perspective is to always remember that you are interviewing the company as much as the company is interviewing you.

Here is how I handled one interview for a sales job. After several interviews, all within the same day, I had reached the position of being one of two final candidates that would meet with the top decision-maker. This was his first hire since joining the company, and I knew he had been regularly rejecting final candidates for months. Meeting with him felt like going to see the Wizard in the *Wizard of Oz*. The big corner office in New York could have been intimidating, but I chose to remain centered and believe that if I was suppose to have this job, it would be evident to both of us. He told me he asked the same question to all the salespeople he interviewed and had not been happy with their answers. The question was "What makes you different from everyone else? Everyone says they have great relationships with their clients so give me something else."

After thinking for a moment, I said, "I enjoy the thrill of getting people excited about saying yes to what I am selling. I know how to make this easy for the buyer because they feel like they are getting a good product at a fair price and have been treated with respect."

I found out later that the other finalist froze and couldn't come up with an answer. I had simply answered from my heart, without thought as to what the *correct* answer might be, and I won the job. So if you are not comfortable thinking on your feet because you get knotted up under pressure, practice this ten-second affirmation and you will tap into the basic truth that the only right answer is the one that comes straight from your heart. Here is the *self-talk* I use:

"When I speak from my heart, I say the right thing, in the right tone, at the right time."

As the interview wound down, I summarized what he said he was looking for and how I fit his criteria. Since we both were aware of the selling process, I laughingly said, "Here's my favorite part. What else, if anything, do you need to know to feel comfortable hiring me?" Note the use of the word "feel." I knew to use this kind of "feelings" questioning because the interviewer (the buyer, if you will, in this case) had expressed in multiple ways that he made his decisions from his gut. For example, at one point, he said, "I want to wake up in the morning and *feel comfortable* that the person I hire is taking initiative without me having to micromanage them." Even if he wasn't the textbook example of a "Feelings" person, I still believe that most people buy with their emotions and then justify the decision with facts.

As a sales professional, you need to ask for the business. In any situation where you are asked to prove that you're the right choice, you need to ask for the job. If he had any objections to hiring me, now was the time to find out what they were and respond to them. (If more time was needed to discuss my hire with his staff, then asking, "What is the next step?" would have become the key question.) I asked for the job by posing this question, "If everyone else agrees on hiring me, can I count on your support too?" He happily told me "yes" and that his search was over. He now had the peace of mind that he had found someone with passion and persistence, not to mention the skills and confidence to close the deal.

In this chapter, you have learned to see the power that occurs when you acquire insight into what the buyer wants and also know how to deliver your message with personal passion. Combining these two elements, you can now make compelling presentations. Here is an affirmation to help you focus on this process:

AFFIRMATION
"I relax into the flow of things, knowing when to speak and when to listen."

Keep in mind that even with all the preparations in the world, there are times when a presentation may go horribly wrong. Here's one that happened to me, and how I handled it.

My magazine publisher was flying from New York to Seattle, and I was flying to Seattle from Los Angeles for a 9:00 a.m. meeting with Nordstrom department store on Monday. All of the details had been confirmed late Friday afternoon with the client. The buying criteria had been defined, and the presentation was ready. This took place back in 1992, so slides were still considered high tech. I even made sure I had a spare bulb and felt good that I was as emotionally ready as I was practically prepared.

The morning of our appointment, we arrived ten minutes early so we could set up our slide projector. We were informed that there was an emergency, and the top decision-maker we were scheduled to see would not be able to meet with us after all. Instead, we would meet with a mid-management employee. This upset my publisher, since he had specifically flown in to meet with the head honcho. Considering this major setback, the publisher advised me to go through the slides as quickly as possible since the person we were meeting with did not have the clout to make an executive decision. In my experience, there is nothing worse than having to rush through anything.

When we got into the conference room, I discovered another problem—this was the smallest meeting room I had ever seen. There were no windows. When you pulled a chair out from the conference table, it hit the wall. Because the room was so small, the distance from the slide projector to the wall was barely sufficient for the slides to be in focus. I started the presentation and was going through it quickly. I came upon one slide that had quotes from other retailers touting the great results they had received by advertising in the magazine. I couldn't read the quotes because the type was so small and barely in focus. I had never bothered to memorize the quotes because I had always been able to read them. I quickly passed over the slide when the publisher said, "Wait, go back and read those quotes."

If I pulled the slide projector back, it would provide just enough distance for those quotes to come into focus. As I started to lift the slide projector, my foot slipped and the image went on the ceiling! By now I was sweating. In a last ditch effort to save the situation I said, "This information, including a copy of all the slides, is in the packet we plan on leaving behind. We can review the quotes when the lights come on."

Needless to say, I was glad when that presentation was over. The key thing I learned from this meeting gone wrong was to focus on being centered, even during times of great stress, by recognizing that I had done my best to prepare for the meeting and not beating myself up later. I was able to use this *self-talk* to stay in a positive state of mind. I needed to keep it together because I had filled my day with other important sales calls with my boss, the publisher, in tow. Just as an Olympic skater may fall in competition, the true champions get up and keep trying to skate their best. If you fall in your presentation, get up and focus on the next call. Focusing on mistakes will only distract you from doing your best in the moment.

The time to analyze your mistake is during down time—that evening, the next day or the following weekend. In order to keep going as best you can, stay focused in the moment. Realize that there are unexpected things that happen, and that only you have the power to rise above them.

Quick Summary of Your Sales Flight Plan:

Secret 1

Your thoughts create your reality.

Your thoughts create your beliefs, which create your actions, which create your habits, which create your character.

Sales come to you from sources expected and unexpected.

Secret 2

Compassion creates rapport.

Recognize and react to personality types: Feeling, Information, Big Picture.

Be a co-pilot with your buyers.

Secret 3

Show you care and buyers will share.

Employ the four benefits for gaining the buyer's criteria: Save them time, make their job easier, make the buyer look good to their boss and make the sales process fun.

Personal passion makes the difference.

Have you ever welcomed a buyer's objections? Would you like to learn how to stay relaxed even when you feel you are not going to get the sale? What is the best way to prevent the buyer from bringing up more objections after you answered the first one? Chapter 4 will answer these questions and more!

Chapter 4
Persistence Pays Off

"When one door closes, another opens; but, often we look so long at the closed door, we do not see the one that has opened for us."
— Helen Keller

Persistence Pays Off

He was born in absolute poverty and was considered "homely" and "gawky" by his peers. When he was 9 years old, he was kicked in the head by a horse and left for dead, but ultimately recovered. Later that same year, his mother died. At the age of 22, he became a store clerk. Though the job barely paid enough to scrape by financially, the owner allowed him to live in the storeroom. To improve himself, he taught himself mathematics and started reading Shakespeare.

When that store went out of business, he borrowed money and bought a store of his own. A year later, that store failed, and he was now saddled with debt. He was elected captain by the ranks of the volunteer company of soldiers he joined during the Black Hawk War of 1832. Soon after the war ended, he tried to capitalize on his popularity by campaigning for a seat in the Illinois House of Representatives—he lost. He had fallen in love for the first time, but his girlfriend fell ill and died when she was only 22 years old. Though devastated by the loss, he began studying law.

On his next attempt, he was elected to the Illinois legislature, but he found himself fighting bouts of debilitating depression. He encountered a new love interest, but she rejected him. Still, he kept searching for love, met a woman named Mary and became engaged. After a long and sometimes turbulent courtship, they were finally married.

Three years into their marriage, they had the first of four sons. The new father's political career took off, and he was elected to the United States Congress. Though he suffered many devastating personal hardships (only the eldest of his four sons lived past the age of 18), his political career continued to flourish, and in 1860 he was elected President of the United States. Abraham Lincoln's life was spent meeting the challenges presented to him—from his wife's descent into mental illness at the loss of her sons to defending our country against political implosion during the Civil War—head on. Lincoln's honesty, compassion and persistence are not only hallmarks of his *character*, but also his legacy as a modern role model.

How often do you feel like giving up when you're faced with obstacles? How many objections can you hear while still maintaining enthusiasm for the product you are selling? Would you like to learn how to get past objections and rejection, to ultimately succeed?

Let's look at what is going on during the sales process and see objections for what they really are.

When someone says "no," it often means, "I'm not convinced yet," rather than, "I'll never say yes." If someone says that the price is too high, it may mean they don't see the underlying value. All of these objections can be looked at as buying signals that indicate that the natural course of the sale has begun. Instead of fearing objections, you can get to the point, in both skill and confidence, where you seek them out, focus on them individually and deal with them head on. Remember that people buy emotionally and then back it up rationally.

To deal with obstacles, both personally and professionally, remember this:

Three Simple Steps for Dealing With Objections

1) See them as a buying signal—welcome them. Let go of your fear of objections.

2) Restate them in your own words and ask for confirmation that you heard them correctly.

3) Ask if there are any other concerns—get them all out in the open so they don't keep coming up after you address the first one.

Let's take a look at each of these in a little more detail:

Step 1—

In almost every case, the irrational fear of objections—as well as trying to be clairvoyant on their motivations—is far worse than taking the risk to find out firsthand. From a spiritual perspective, fear is experienced when you feel alone or under attack. It often stems from being disconnected from your spiritual self and without your usual means of support. Metaphorically, you can think of this situation as like being a drop of water being separated from the ocean. The drop is not powerful by itself, but cumulatively all the drops can create a veritable tidal wave. When you remember that rejection does not diminish your self-worth, you are able to transcend fearing it.

Remember that your thoughts create your reality. When you reframe your fear by seeing an objection as a buying signal, then you will respond to it in a completely different manner. It's helpful to realize that fear can be at work on both sides of the table. Most people *want* to buy, but are afraid of making the wrong decision. Their fear gets expressed as an objection. If you, as the seller, fear objections, then what you have is fear meeting fear. This creates a stalemate. Worse yet, fear from the buyer can easily mask itself in anger, apathy and irrationality.

If you let selling come from a place of fear, here are some of the other things that can happen. Your fear that in letting the buyer talk, you will lose control of the meeting. This causes you to dominate the conversation. Your fear that the buyer won't like you may trigger overcompensation or boorishness. Your fear that the buyer is ready to end the meeting at any moment can result in desperation to get to the punchline sooner, so you rush to the close, disrupting the rhythm of the meeting and losing the sale.

But if you approach these situations with compassion, the buyer will feel like his needs are being acknowledged and therefore, he is in a safe place to let go of his fear. Once you both let go of your individual fears, the sales flight will take off, and you can be co-pilots together. Removing your half of the fear equation allows you to focus on the buyer's anxiety and move the process forward.

Step 2—

Listen to the buyer with your ears, see their point of view with your eyes and open your heart to what they are feeling. When people feel that you are truly understanding what they are saying, as well as what they are feeling, they will respect and trust you. If you respond to an objection by adapting a defensive posture, it will simply heighten the buyer's fear and serve to create an adversarial relationship. Often times, just restating the buyer's objection will make the buyer feel validated. Once the buyer can trust that you have heard and understand their objections, then you can begin to respond to them.

Step 3—

After a buyer has expressed whatever objection they might have, ask if there is "anything else." These two simple words can work magic. Often the opposition is more of a knee-jerk reaction rather than a potential deal breaker, but fear of an imagined deluge of objections keeps the seller from investigating closer. The pattern I have noticed in my many years as a successful seller is that if you don't ask for all of the objections up front, then you risk countering one and instead of going straight to asking for the order, you only get another objection. Around and around you go with both the seller and buyer getting increasingly defensive and frustrated. Another option that I recommend is encouraging the buyer to tell you as many objections as they can as early in the process as possible. Then ask the buyer for the business by getting an agreement that if the objections are all met, you will have a deal.

With the knowledge of the specific objections and thoughtfully crafted answers, you can show how your product fits their needs. One mistake that many salespeople make is that they don't recognize that often the need that is not being met is a personal one. For instance, the buyer may need to feel important or valued. If that's the case, then you might try what I do when I'm talking to a media buyer at an ad agency. These buyers are under tremendous pressure to keep their client happy and from defecting to a competing agency. I tell them that I see that a big part of my job is to make them look good to their client. With that established, any objections are voiced in a way that we are on the same team, working for the same goal, with the best interest of their client as our mutual motivation.

Of all the things you can do to aid in your own long-term success in sales, no matter what the product, one of the most important is to never take the rejection personally. The power to deflect professional rejection must come from within you. If you don't judge or reject yourself, a negative opinion or setback will not deflate your self-esteem. This is the basis for:

Secret #4

True self-esteem is not defined by the results of one sale or one event.

A great metaphor for this comes from writer and speaker Dr. Wayne Dyer, author of the bestseller *There is a Spiritual Solution to Every Problem*. He said that when you squeeze an orange, you get orange juice. It doesn't matter what time of day or where you squeeze, you always get orange juice. So, the relevant question here becomes what happens when someone puts the squeeze on you? Do they get kindness and patience? Or do they get anger and fear? The goal is to have your patience and compassion come out no matter what the circumstance, just as certainly as extracting orange juice from an orange.

Now that we have addressed the spiritual basis of handling objections, here are a few practical ways to handle them.

One method that has worked well for me is to list the top three most common objections I receive and develop solid answers to each of them. By doing this, I feel cool, confident and prepared, and being prepared relegates the *surprise objection* to the category of just another familiar bump in the road. Instead of being defensive with an objection, I can respond with compassion and logic.

You can also help your cause by leading into your response with a carefully worded phrase that puts the buyers at ease. Here is an example of how to do that: "Many of my best customers had the same feeling at first and what they have found is…"

This opening response to a common objection will allow the buyer to feel that you heard them and that you are not implying that they are wrong or out of place for voicing their hesitation. To a common objection, such as price, you could offer, "Many people feel that way at first, and they have found that the tangible response they receive to advertising in the magazine makes the premium price worth every penny."

To further highlight the power of this methodology, here is an example of how to overcome objections in the job market using the three simple steps outlined above. Several years ago, I was interviewing at a magazine that charged advertisers a premium rate compared to its competitors. They wanted to hire a salesperson that could quantify for potential advertisers the value of its readership to justify the higher rates they charged.

After I had presented my strategy on how I would create value for the magazine, they gave me an offer to start at a salary that was below my requirements. I said to the person handling the negotiation that the offer reminded me of buying a home. (This is something many people can relate to through personal experience or the experience of friends.) When shopping for a house or condo, a buyer often makes a wish list of amenities that helps to justify the purchase price—a view, a pool, a good location, etc. Often it turns out you have to pay more than what you planned in order to get everything on your list. Otherwise, you give up the view or the pool and settle for something less.

When the interviewer agreed that this was indeed a similar process, I said, "I'm the house with the view, the pool and the great location. If you want a salesperson that meets all of the items on your wish list, you will have to pay a little more. After all, if I can't convince you that I'm worth more than the average sales rep, how can I ever convince an advertiser that a page in your magazine is worth more than one in the competition?" (I got the job and at the salary I wanted.)

Later, I learned from the person who hired me that I was the first person they interviewed out of 30 candidates. (During the time between the first and final interview, I kept sending in ideas on how I would approach certain clients. By acting as if I was already on the team, they came to the conclusion that it made sense to hire me.) They told me they ended up buying the first house they saw. So whether you are the first, middle or final candidate, you can always get the job if you believe in yourself and your own worth.

To illustrate an effective way of even overcoming common, everyday objections, let me share another personal story. Have you ever felt like you were interviewing for the right to get a table at a nice restaurant? Sometimes it can feel just as intimidating as a job interview. Here is an example of how I didn't take the first "no" as the final answer.

One evening a friend and I found ourselves with an hour to spare before the show we were seeing was scheduled to start. We decided to have a quick dinner at a restaurant across the street. When we walked in, we were told there was a two-hour wait for a table. I then asked about the possibility of sitting at the bar and eating. I quickly received a second "no." I was told they didn't serve food at the bar. I noticed one empty table in the bar/lobby entrance. I asked if we could sit there, instead of the main dining room. Soon my friend and I were sitting down having a wonderful meal that finished in time for our show. My friend pointed out to me how I kept coming back with different ideas and suggestions every time the maitre d' raised an objection. My friend said she would have stopped after the first "no." This story speaks to my point that once you stop fearing rejection, you open yourself up to seeing additional possibilities.

If you keep coming up with possible solutions, you increase your chances of getting a "yes." You can't keep asking for the same thing in the same way. You need to present different options in order to overcome an objection.

The combination of persistence and creativity is the same, whether it is getting a table at a restaurant or getting a client to say yes. For over five years, I had been calling on Nike® to advertise.

They have always had two main objections: premium rates in comparison to other magazines and the fact that the median age of our reader is older than the audience they target. Year after year, I continued to address these concerns by showing the value of our readers and how our readers lead active lifestyles, in spite of their chronological age. In sales, one of the biggest challenges is how to spend your time and effort efficiently, without giving up.

Then one year, their strategy expanded and they wanted to target a new demographic. The new focus happened to fit our strength of reaching influential designers and trendsetters. And after several meetings and presentations, we were able to finally get that business. So you see, just because the buyer's parameters don't fit today, doesn't mean they never will. However, if you cease to engage the prospect, you will never see the opportunity to overcome the objections. Sales truly do come from sources both expected and unexpected, if you stay in the game and allow yourself to be open to the possibility.

Here is a quote that applies whether you are selling yourself for a job or selling a product or service. Sarah Baime wrote it during America's economic depression in 1935.

"Success is failure turned inside out—
The silver tint of the clouds of doubt—
And you never can tell how close you are,
It may be near when it seems afar;
So stick to the fight when you're hardest hit—
It's when things seem worst that you mustn't quit."

Now when you hear an objection, here is an affirmation to say to yourself:

AFFIRMATION

"I welcome with inner calm and confidence any and all objections as a buying signal. I listen with an open heart and respond with the right words that give the best results for all parties."

Quick Summary of Your Sales Flight Plan:

Secret 1

Your thoughts create your reality.

Your thoughts create your beliefs, which create your actions, which create your habits, which create your character.

Sales come to you from sources expected and unexpected.

Secret 2

Compassion creates rapport.

Recognize and react to personality types: Feeling, Information, Big Picture.

Be a co-pilot with your buyers.

Secret 3

Show you care and buyers will share.

Employ the four benefits for gaining the buyer's criteria: Save them time, make their job easier, make the buyer look good to their boss and make the sales process fun.

Personal passion makes the difference.

Secret 4

See an objection as a buying signal—let go of your fear and the buyer will let go of theirs.

Listen to the buyer with your ears, see their point of view with your eyes and open your heart to what they are feeling.

Ask for all the objections and ask for the business, too.

Don't let your self-esteem be defined by one sale or event.

Have you ever been obsessed with winning? Do you often worry about the competition? Are you constantly comparing yourself and coming up short? Chapter 5 will show you how to resolve these all-too-common energy zappers.

Chapter 5
Rising Above the Competition

"There are no passengers on spaceship Earth.
We are all crew."

— Marshall McLuhan

Rising Above the Competition

After years of training, the day of the big statewide qualifying meet had arrived. The swimmers were arranged to compete in heats based on their fastest time. Our swimmer was placed in the final heat of six, out of a total of thirty-six swimmers from across the state. A Mark Spitz look-alike with the fastest trial time was seated right next to him in the back row. As our swimmer watched the five rows ahead of him compete, he kept telling himself, "I can win this race." He noticed the Mark Spitz look-alike kept glancing around, trying to "psych out" the other swimmers by flexing his muscles and taking loud, deep breaths. In order to overcome the butterflies he was starting to experience, our swimmer decided to tune out all the distractions and keep focused on visualizing his own race.

As he climbed up on the starting block, a wave of energy surged through his body. "This is it," he said to himself. "I am going to swim faster than I ever have before, and I am going to win!" The official told the swimmers to take their marks, then BANG. The gun signaling the race went off

69

quickly, followed by a loud whistle. This meant one of the swimmers had literally, "jumped the gun." A false start by one means all of the swimmers have to get back up on the blocks. If a swimmer does this twice, he is disqualified. Regardless of who the perpetrator is, a false start can often make it hard for a swimmer to get his concentration back. Undaunted, the swimmer said to himself, "Well, at least I know how cold the water is now."

A second BANG and this time they were off for real. It was a short 50-meter race, so every one hundredth of a second mattered. (The touchpad at the end of the race measures each swimmer's time to that decimal.) Under the water, the swimmer could hear the roar of the crowd. As the swimmer finished the first of the two laps, he said to himself, "Touch the wall and make a quick turn." As he approached the wall for the finish, he gave it everything he had without knowing whether he had won or not. What this swimmer did know is that he had given it his personal best.

In a few seconds, the results were posted. Our swimmer had won! And that swimmer was me (many years ago when I competed on my varsity high school swim team). I found out later that the Mark Spitz look-alike, who had beaten me in every other race, made one fatal error. Instead of lifting his head straight out of the water to take a breath, he looked sideways to see if I was ahead or behind him. This wasted energy slowed him down just enough for me to beat him.

That race taught me a valuable lesson:

Secret #5

Focus on your own progress and you will win.

Recently my 8-year-old godson, Max, came home from school and told his Mom he felt like a loser. When she asked him why, he said that in gym class he always came in last in the running races. She offered to get a stopwatch and time him to see if he could improve. When I heard this story, I offered to have my trainer Jay Kerwin, a former Air Force Reserve Commando, give him a private session. For Max, just knowing that he had a trainer who could help him instantly improved his mood.

On the day of the training, Jay asked Max to run as fast as he could across the field. After Max ran, Jay said, "Was that really as fast as you can go?" Max shrugged and said, "I guess so." Jay said "On a scale of 1-10, what would you give it?" Max didn't understand the concept, so Jay showed Max what running at *level 7* looks like for Jay. Then Jay said, "This is what running at *level 10* looks like." He put on put on his *10 face* and gave it all he had. From seeing Jay's example, Max then ran at his *level 10* and was much faster.

Jay suggested to Max that the only reason he was coming in last in school was that Max wasn't giving it a *10* effort. He told Max the secret to running is confidence. When I saw Max a week later, he asked me if I wanted to race (something he had never done before). He was quite a bit faster. He said "Uncle John, you know the secret to running is confidence, don't you?" I said, "Yes, Max, it's the secret to everything."

When you put on your *10 face* in selling, you are focusing on your own progress. So what else can you focus on instead of what the competition is doing? Is there more to successful selling than hitting your sales goal? How can you win by making yourself better, instead of wasting your energy making the competition look bad?

For a sales professional, the standard way of thinking is to focus on how to achieve your sales goal. Often, building market share is considered just as important as meeting your specific sales goals. Whatever you focus on takes up your energy. But there is an irony here. If a buyer feels you are only focused on your own personal goals, or on cutting down the competition, they may feel you don't value their goals.

There is an alternate way to think about hitting your numbers—and the buyer's needs. Focus on your sales goals *and* visualize how achieving them can also help your buyers. This is a powerful combination for success. It allows you to remain focused on your own goals while also incorporating what the buyer needs. When you help buyers meet their goals, yours will be met, too.

Here's how I look at this combination in my job. When I sell an ad, my clients' sales go up, and then they can employ more people to make and sell their products. When you see what you are doing in sales as part of a bigger picture, it helps you see the valuable contribution you make in your life and to all the lives around you. This allows you to focus your energy on your strengths and not waste it worrying about what the competition is offering.

When you realize that cooperation can replace competition and still bring you success, you see your sales life in a different way. Recently an advertiser asked one of my competitors and I if we would join forces to produce an event. Instead of having two medium-sized events (one from each of us), they wanted to have one large event with both of us pooling our resources. My competitor and I agreed to do this in the interest of making the advertiser happy. Our willingness to work together in the spirit of cooperation greatly enhanced our reputation with the advertiser. The joint event was a success and as a result, the company increased its commitment of ad pages to both publications.

Focusing on your own game can mean more than just working to get competitors to cooperate. It can also include putting together non-competing companies as partners. Here is one successful idea that had more positive ripples emanating from it than anything I could have imagined.

In 2000, the president of the Academy of Television Arts & Sciences contacted a producer at *Entertainment Tonight*, looking for input on how they could increase publicity for their annual awards. The idea was to improve ratings for the show by doing something to create a buzz before the actual event. The Academy president suggested having a fashion show honoring the costume designers who had been nominated for an award that year. By having celebrities model in the show, *Entertainment Tonight* would naturally want to cover it. Since the TV Academy had never produced a fashion show before, they knew that by joining forces with a fashion magazine, which produces fashion shows all the time, they would have more credibility with the press. The producer at *Entertainment Tonight* suggested that our magazine be included, in addition to the other two magazines they were already considering.

I met with the president of the TV Academy to discuss what we could bring to the event. By asking one key question, I discovered an opening that became the start of a successful partnership. The question I asked was, "What type of jewelry do you have planned for the celebrity fashion show?" While the designers for the clothes had been selected, the role of jewelry had not yet been considered.

One of my advertisers, a jewelry company, had a goal of getting celebrities to wear platinum to award shows. They believed that when people see celebrities wearing platinum jewelry to these kinds of events, sales would go up. The suggestion to include the jewelry company as a co-sponsor of the fashion show secured our partnership with the TV Academy for the event.

From a series of meetings, we developed the concept of producing an editorial supplement on how TV influenced fashion trends over the years. The jewelry company would sponsor the editorial supplement with ads from their jewelry designers. Also, they would supply jewelry for the celebrity models to wear at the fashion show and at the awards show. The supplement was polybagged with our June issue. Additionally, the TV Academy allowed our magazine and jeweler's supplement to be polybagged with their magazine, which went to all of their voting members—actors, producers, directors and others in the world of television. Another value-added bonus to this collaboration benefited the magazine itself: by working with the TV Academy's magazine editors, our editors were given access to their incredible archive of still photographs from the entire history of modern TV.

Not only did *Entertainment Tonight* help publicize the event, but *E! Entertainment Television* covered it as a half-hour special and included an interview with the president of the jewelry company. The media buzz continued even after the fashion show. Katie Couric, from the *Today* show, interviewed our entertainment editor—with the editor wearing the pair of earrings that the jewelry company had loaned her, of course—about the TV/fashion supplement concept. The *Today* show took the still photo images from the supplement and brought them to life with actual clips from the different TV shows.

While the value of the publicity for the magazine from this exposure is itself incalculable, we further benefited by becoming the only magazine to get these platinum ads. But what is crucial to remember is that everybody who participated in the event won. The TV Academy got what it wanted:

The awards show received increased buzz, press exposure and subsequently experienced some of their highest ratings for the telecast in years. The jewelry company was thrilled that they got the primetime media exposure (and the association with celebrities and the awards) that they had been seeking.

Beyond the practical benefits of working together, the very act of cooperation can bring you peace of mind instead of anxiety by allowing you to stop focusing on being better than everyone else and begin focusing on being better than you were yesterday. And that shift in perspective can make all the difference! Harmony always sounds sweeter to the human ear than cacophony.

A key factor to remember is what Jesuit priest Pierre Tielhard De Chardin said, "We are spiritual beings having a human experience not human beings having a spiritual experience." As such, you can focus on your creativity and doing this will infuse your life with positive momentum. Instead of falling victim to your primal fears of what the competition is doing, you can sell from a place of inner confidence. When you allow yourself to believe that you are more than just the sum of what you physically experience (through the five senses), you can begin to sell with genuine enthusiasm and integrity.

If you accept that in sales, as in life, your real competition is actually yourself, you give yourself permission to keep growing and facing challenges that lead you beyond your comfort zone. For example, for many sales professionals, giving the same sales pitch over and over breeds a kind of complacency. When you are first learning to use a new sales technique or new set of data, you have to actually think about what you're saying instead of being on mental auto-pilot—and that can be scary or exciting depending on who you are. When you overcome your fear of trying something new, you expand your comfort zone and your whole universe.

Have you ever felt like a deer in the headlights? How can you use your thoughts to overcome fear and try something new? Are you willing to stretch out and overcome your fear? If you are, one of the best ways to accomplish this is to channel your competitive spirit into learning new selling techniques and coming up with new ways to help your buyers. This is what keeps life—not mention the sales process—fresh and exciting.

Consider that learning to fly a plane (or even being in one as a passenger) is about overcoming your fear of leaving the security of the ground. If you just do what you have always done—such as staying in a safe place even when it isn't working very well—you will never broaden your current perspective and take a leap of faith that will bring your happiness and your successes to a new level.

It was exactly this desire to shake things up a little that led me to go skydiving. Not only did I have to overcome my fear of taking off in a small plane, but I also had to take myself one GIANT step further and trust that the parachute would open on my way back to the ground. Since skydiving had always been a desire of mine, I "jumped" at the opportunity to share the adventure with some friends. Not only was I no longer putting off something I had always wanted to do, but also the experience of gently floating to the earth gave me an actual physical sensation of being safe when I burst through my fears. Once you have faced and mastered your fears, you can leave the ground (or existing patterns) and return to them in a new way with a completely different perspective.

When you learn that your greatest ally and your greatest adversary in life is yourself, you gain the knowledge that time is best spent growing your skills alongside your spiritual instincts, instead of nursing your animal fears. As you give up the controls that you have let rule your life, you will grow into a new, higher place of calm and peace. The result? You take off. Just as a student pilot learns that using his experience and confidence is just as important as learning the uses of all of the controls in the cockpit, it is possible to use the tools that you may have forgotten that you have—just like that pilot—to bring your own special touch to the flight.

AFFIRMATION

"I am always making progress on the road to success. I stay focused on my own results and growth."

Often, salespeople can get distracted from their own progress by listening to other people talk about obstacles that they believe are coming their way, such as the current state of the economy—good, bad or unstable as it may be. The key here is to remember that you can choose whether to give power to external factors—like the day's news or the latest hiccup in the stock market—or not. My point is simple. Wealth of every imaginable dimension comes from within.

Since you create your reality, you can either wallow in the negative *self-talk* examples used in Chapter One such as:

"The economy is down."
"No one is buying now."
"My competitors have better products and pricing."

Or you can transform the negativity into something more positive by thinking like the winner you are:

"I prosper in all economic situations."
"What I have to offer is what people need all the time."
"I come up with ideas and solutions that give my products value."

Remember that negative thoughts can be like wire hangers in your closet—you let a few in and the next thing you know, you have a closet full of them. By focusing on positive thoughts, you will see true power in the results you achieve.

Quick Summary of Your Sales Flight Plan:

Secret 1

Your thoughts create your reality.

Your thoughts create your beliefs, which create your actions, which create your habits, which create your character.

Sales come to you from sources expected and unexpected.

Secret 2

Compassion creates rapport.

Recognize and react to personality types: Feeling, Information, Big Picture.

Be a co-pilot with your buyers.

Secret 3

Show you care and buyers will share.

Employ the four benefits for gaining the buyer's criteria: Save them time, make their job easier, make the buyer look good to their boss and make the sales process fun.

Personal passion makes the difference.

Secret 4

See an objection as a buying signal—let go of your fear and the buyer will let go of theirs.

Listen to the buyer with your ears, see their point of view with your eyes and open your heart to what they are feeling.

Ask for all the objections and ask for the business, too.

Don't let your self-esteem be defined by one sale or event.

Secret 5

Focus on your own progress and you will win.

Cooperation can replace competition.

Compete with yourself and expand your comfort zone.

Have you ever wondered how to increase the number of sales you are able to close without feeling pushy or aggressive? Do you feel nervous or unworthy asking for the sale? Would you like to learn ways to make closing a sale easier? Chapter 6 shows you how to do this and more!

Chapter 6
Relax into Yes

"To accomplish great things, we must not only act,
but also dream; not only plan, but also believe."
— Anatole France

Since their youth, two athletes had trained with the hope of one day winning an Olympic gold medal. When they met in the figure skating finals, the athlete who had won medals in the past was the odds-on favorite. The other skater was a young newcomer and thought to have potential for future games, at best. Because she wasn't ranked at the top, the younger athlete skated before the champion. Without the pressure facing the favorite, she chose to make her moment in the spotlight about the joy of skating and not about winning. She skated from a place of inner calm and strength. She nailed every jump and, with each success, won the audience over a little bit more. In turn, she became inspired by the crowd's support. The smile on her face radiated with the love she had of her sport and, at the end of her program, she received not only a standing ovation but also her best scores to date.

Then the reigning champion took to the ice. You could see the pressure on her face and in every muscle of her body.

But, as befitting the seasoned pro she was, she skated well—hitting all her jumps but one. However, her performance clearly lacked the newcomer's sheer joy of skating. But that one error—and perhaps her own fear of flying—cost Michelle Kwan the gold medal and a new champion was born. Sarah Hughes, in a surprise upset, won the gold medal at the 2002 Winter Games.

In the sales arena, you may have developed rapport, gained insight into the buyer's criteria, given your presentation with passion and overcome objections; but if you don't close the sale, you can't win the gold. Just as winning the skating competition came down to feeling the sheer joy of participation in the event to close the deal, you will need to feel the same joy to soar across the finish line. So, what does it take for you to soar across the finish line? Where can you find your joy, unencumbered by the stress of having to win? The answers lie within.

The practice of meditation has been shown to be a great way to clear your mind and find inspiration. When we quiet our thoughts of fear and doubt, we make room for inspiration to come to us. The same is true in the sales process, when it's time to ask for the sale. If we are uncomfortable with the silence that someone else needs to make a decision, we will have the tendency to crowd the buyer with our own thoughts and not give them the space they need to arrive at the right decision. There is a big difference between someone saying, "I want to think about it"—which is an objection usually meaning they don't have enough information—and someone taking 30 seconds to give you an answer. That momentary silence is not the time to give more information. If you do, you may well miss the opportunity to let the buyer *relax into yes*.

For example, let's say you are selling a house. You ask the buyers if they want to make an offer. During the silence while the buyers are thinking, you become anxious and say, "How about if I throw in the refrigerator? Will you take it then?" At that point, you have not only lost the opportunity for the buyers to say yes, but have given them new information (which they may interpret as "the house isn't really worth the price on the table") and the process has to start all over again.

Secret #6

When you quiet the thoughts in your mind, you can be comfortable with the silence in the room.

The rhythm of a good sales call should feel natural. And the most natural thing you do is breathe. One of the best ways to become aware of your breathing is to meditate. For some, this may evoke images of sitting for hours in an uncomfortable position with votive candles lit all around. But this is not necessarily what meditation means in the sales process. Simply quieting your mind—even if it is only for ten seconds—after asking for the sale, is a form of mediation. And at the end of this chapter, I will share with you a key affirmation to achieve this quiet state.

By feeling comfortable with silence, you avoid the urge to start talking and making the buyer feel nervous or rushed. Talking non-stop during a sales call is like exhaling continually without ever pausing to draw a breath. The result is vertigo for all concerned. Here is an example of how I used a ten-second meditation to relax with unexpected results. Recently, I went to a restaurant with a friend after rollerblading. We were told it would be over an hour for a table. This shouldn't have surprised us. It was a Saturday night and the restaurant was not only popular, but offered a panoramic view of the ocean. I took a deep breath and told myself that I was willing to relax into the moment and not be in a hurry. That ten-second thought worked for me. To my delight, I found my friend, normally a double *A* type personality, was also in the same relaxed mode. We asked to wait at the bar, but there were no seats available. We ended up perching on a windowsill and found ourselves quite content to look out at the ocean and enjoy our drinks. After watching the sunset, we had the excitement of the unexpected moment—we saw a pod of dolphin swim by the window. Had we not been willing to wait, we would have missed this beautiful sight. Back at work, it occurred to me that although things don't always happen in the time frame we expect, our needs somehow are inevitably met. The key is remembering that the right things happen in the right time.

Abraham Maslow, the psychologist known for his theories on self-actualization, said, "If the only tool in your tool-box is a hammer, then you tend to start looking for nails to hit." In the same vein, if you only have a hammer to convince someone to say yes, then you won't be as successful as someone who has many more tools in his toolbox, including the ability to be comfortable with silence.

A few years back, I was calling on Gump's in San Francisco to propose that they start advertising jewelry, as well as their home decorating products. The Vice President of Marketing said that he felt our rates for an ad were too high. I said, "If you sell just one piece of this $40,000 jewelry that you are advertising, you will have more than paid for the cost of the ad." Then I waited to see his reaction. I had many other ideas and reasons why he should buy, but something inside me told me just to let him digest this concept. He looked down, for what was about 20 seconds—to me, it felt like 20 minutes. When he looked up, he said, "I never thought of it like that. Let's do it." Had I not given him the time to process this new information, I would not have received the order.

Would you like to let the excitement of the unexpected moment allow the buyer the space needed to say yes? Or do you bombard clients with information to force a sale?

One way to become more comfortable during that silence is to use this ten-second meditation:

MEDITATION

"I am comfortable during silence.
I am patient."

So what does it take to go from "no" to "yes?" To make that leap happen, the first thing to know is where you are in the sales process. Once you get your bearings, you can move fluidly from one stage to the next. By the time you have established rapport, identified the buyer's needs and key buying criteria, shown how your product meets those needs and overcome as many objections as possible, then and only then is it time to finally get your "yes."

If all of the above stages have taken place, you should think of getting to "yes" as the logical, almost inevitable next step. To put it another way: at the end of the flight that you jointly planned with the buyer, the expected conclusion is a smooth landing. It is a goal and expectation that the buyer and seller as co-pilots should have been building from the beginning. The smooth landing is not the result of a forced tug of war, but rather the calm, mutually desired conclusion.

The mantra of *old school* selling is that the seller should *always be closing*. This implies that the seller should always be pushing the buyer for a decision. A fresher, more partnership-oriented approach is *always be kind* and *always be connected*. The ultimate win/win takes place when you have worked with your buyer to develop a deal so harmonious with the buyer's needs that, on a practical level, the buyer's only possible answer is yes.

When that time comes, you still need to know *how* to ask. Just as Chapter Two discussed the three different types of personalities related to rapport building, there are different ways to sail into a smooth closing for each personality type. Here is a general question and an example you could use when selling a house for each:

1. Feeling Personality:

Ask them questions like, "Does this feel comfortable to you?" "Can you sense how happy you will be in your new home?"

2. Information Personality:

Ask them questions like, "Does this all add up?" "Do the numbers make sense, in terms of your getting value for this house?"

3. Big Picture Personality:

Ask them questions like, "Does this look like a good decision for you?" "Can you imagine how great your new home will look in five years when you've remodeled it and realized its full potential?"

Now you have new tools to use to close the deal. You can feel confident in asking for the sale without feeling pushy. "Yes" is no longer a leap of faith, but something you've earned by partnering with the buyer and connecting on a spiritual level.

Quick Summary of Your Sales Flight Plan:

Secret 1

Your thoughts create your reality.

Your thoughts create your beliefs, which create your actions, which create your habits, which create your character.

Sales come to you from sources expected and unexpected.

Secret 2

Compassion creates rapport.

Recognize and react to personality types: Feeling, Information, Big Picture.

Be a co-pilot with your buyers.

Secret 3

Show you care and buyers will share.

Employ the four benefits for gaining the buyer's criteria: Save them time, make their job easier, make the buyer look good to their boss and make the sales process fun.

Personal passion makes the difference.

Secret 4

See an objection as a buying signal—let go of your fear and the buyer will let go of theirs.

Listen to the buyer with your ears, see their point of view with your eyes and open your heart to what they are feeling.

Ask for all the objections and ask for the business, too.

Don't let your self-esteem be defined by one sale or event.

Secret 5

Focus on your own progress and you will win.

Cooperation can replace competition.

Compete with yourself and expand your comfort zone.

Secret 6

Quiet the thoughts in your mind and you will be comfortable with the silence after asking for the sale.

Closing is a natural result of the sales flight. It is like a plane having a smooth landing.

Remember: ABK—Always Be Kind and ABC-Always Be Connected.

Would you like to learn how to inspire others while staying inspired yourself? Would you like to learn how to show your boss that you care about them as much as you do your buyers? Have you ever wondered how you can pass along your success to others? Chapter 7 will show you how.

Chapter 7
Passing Your Good
along to Others

"If I can stop one heart from breaking,
I shall not live in vain;
If I can ease one life the aching, or cool one pain,
or help one fainting robin unto his nest again
I shall not live in vain."

—Emily Dickinson

Passing Your Good along to Others

r. Wayne Dyer tells a wonderful and insightful story. A farmer had developed the best seeds for a crop of corn that grew taller, heartier and quicker than that of any of his neighbors' crops. The neighboring farmers were shocked when, instead of jealously guarding his secret, he shared his seeds with them. So they asked, "Why would you do this?" And the generous farmer replied, "In order for my crop to be the best it can be, I need all the seeds that may blow into my field from your fields to be at the same superior level of quality. By sharing the seeds with you, we all win." This is an example of literally _passing your good_ on to others and having the results benefit everyone. When you do this in business, with your clients and your co-workers, you will add yet another powerful tool to your selling tool kit. And it is both the sense of receiving the abundance around you and giving some of it back that are key to making you feel good about yourself in your work, as well as in your personal life.

In essence, the practice of _giving back_ to replenish the greater good is motivated by your view of the world around you. Do you see it as a fixed pie where if I take a bigger piece, it automatically means your piece is smaller? Or do you see life as an expanding pie, forever growing with its unlimited source of creative ideas and abundant prosperity—much like the ocean has plenty of water for all of us to fill our buckets without seeming to diminish its source? So Secret #7 is Secret #5 taken one step further. Success comes when you concentrate on your own progress. Worrying about someone else taking your good away from you only dilutes your focus and causes delay in reaching your goal. Once you shift to a belief system of unlimited supply, you are able to give freely to others, not only without fear—but also with joy.

Do you remember being excited and a little bit scared on your first day of school? Have you ever started a new job and been so lost that you didn't even know where the bathroom was? Well, if the answer to either of those questions is yes, then you know how comforting it is to find a friendly face among strangers. It's when you make an extra effort and go beyond mere common courtesy that sharing your experiences and good fortune with others takes on a more personal, mentoring quality. I take the opportunity to do this from the very first time I meet a new employee—helping them navigate the corporate landscape, as well as offering encouragement and my own shortcuts to getting things done faster. After all, even if I have only been working somewhere for a week, I still have information that could get them through their first day. As a result of my making an extra effort, I have had the joy of seeing many great business and personal friendships grow from this small act of kindness.

Another opportunity to mentor is by letting someone who is looking for a job, or even new to your field altogether, interview you. It may seem like an imposition on your already busy calendar, but today's job hunter could well be your boss next year or at your next job. In the world of business—as in life, in general—what goes around comes around. The concept of ABK—*Always Be Kind*—applies to yourself, your clients, your co-workers, as well as your fellow human beings who are looking for a job or career advice.

A third way to be a mentor is to share your own personal tricks of the trade with your colleagues. If you discover a successful antidote for a common sales objection, tell the other people on your team. If a fellow salesperson gets a sale, congratulate them on it. The more you give of yourself, the more you will ultimately receive of others.

Finally, mentoring can be as easy as leading by example. For instance, you can be the one to keep morale and optimism alive in the office environment, instead of following the pack into a complaining, critical circle of fear that can appear when the market gets tough. When others see you as calm and successful, they learn that being stressed out and angry is not the best way to achieve their personal and professional goals.

Many successful people have benefited from a mentor's guidance in parts or even throughout their careers. One of the great things about achieving your goals is the path you blaze for someone else.

Mentors are like magnets; people are inherently drawn to their experiences, achievements and reputations because we long for the very same things in our lives. Conversely, when you are the one in need of a little extra guidance, you really begin to appreciate the potential of everyone who crosses your path.

A mentor that has made a huge impact on my life is Alyce Alston, the publisher of *W* magazine. She leads by inspiration. She instills in each member of her team a sense that we have infinite potential to achieve our goals—both individually and as a sum of our parts. She also makes sure everyone treats each other with kindness and respect.

A perfect example of this inspirational leadership occurred when the entire worldwide staff of the magazine was gathered in New York for back-to-back meetings to celebrate the magazine's present gains and plan for those of the future. Alyce realized that scheduling time to give something back to the community is just as important to have on the agenda as the awards that were given to the staff later that evening. One year, we volunteered at "God's Love We Deliver," an AIDS service organization, and either helped prepare food or wrapped presents for the holidays. The next year, we volunteered at a homeless shelter and helped organize donated clothing so that it could be distributed more easily. Not only did these experiences build teamwork, but also the net charitable result of the group effort was exponentially greater than any of us could offer on our own.

With just a little conscious thought, giving back should come naturally to you. Find something or some cause that interests you and volunteer your time, give a little money—or do both! If you love pets, volunteer at a pet shelter. If you are blessed with patience and energy to spare, volunteer at an after-school program targeting children who would otherwise come home to an empty house. If you want to combine business with doing good, then find out what charities are important to your clients and join them in their involvement. This deepens your relationship with your clients, as well as giving you a way to make a contribution. Giving back is like exercise—find something you like to do and do it!

When you start to see your talent in selling as a creative way to help others meet their needs, finding ways to pass your knowledge and enthusiasm along to others becomes a habit. A painter paints to express himself artistically, and a salesperson sells because it is the only way to bring that unique part of them to life. In the same way that an advertising campaign is only deemed successful when it measurably influences the targeted audience, making the effort to improve humanity is the yardstick that charts the spiritual growth that is within each of us.

Once you become a person who delivers support and peace of mind, you can be a resource, not only for your clients, but also for your boss or bosses. Remember that you don't have to be perfect 100% of the time to be successful—just think positive thoughts 51% of the time. It is the sum total of your thoughts which determines the outcome. You can be a resource to your bosses by finding fresh solutions for a problem, rather than just dumping it on them—which is basically like saying, "I can't fly this plane anymore. You take over." Together, you and your boss work as co-pilots to fix it. If you can present your boss with just one possible solution to the problem, you have proven your commitment to a partnership where smoothing out current difficulties and preventing them in the future is part of everyone's pre-flight checklist.

When you think of your boss as a person, and not just in terms of a title, it enables you to put yourself in that position. What kind of stress are they under? How can you make their day better? What can you do for them before they ask? The opportunities are many. Preparing a *State of the Business* report, presenting a new idea that everyone can use or simply sending a thoughtful note are opportunities for you to help them redirect their focus in a positive way.

The same is true if you are the boss. Treating your staff with compassion and support will bring you loyalty, and allow you to attract and retain a team who will go the extra mile for you.

One of the most clear and insightful books on *passing your good* along to others is by Tim Sanders, Chief Solutions Officer at Yahoo! The book is entitled, *Love is the Killer App: How to Win Business and Influence Friends.* When looking for a common denominator, he noticed that the "happiest people and the most successful are smart, generous and kind." He goes on to say, "Buyers don't want to be sold. They want to make educated buying decisions. To make a sale, you must join them on their buying path." Sanders encourages everyone to pass on the knowledge they get from reading books, as a way to increase their network. "The way to win hearts and influence buyers is to express your compassion with your knowledge and network. Compassion is the icing on the excellent cake baked with knowledge and our network."

Here is an affirmation to keep inspiring you to help others:

"I share my thoughts, ideas and guidance with all. When I do, I soar to heights that can't be tracked by radar."

Just as a plane has to stay balanced, despite any outside turbulence, you can maintain your sense of being centered when your actions and thoughts stem from the purity of the heart. When you integrate your personal and spiritual beliefs with all aspects of your identity, you allow your heart to gives you an inner peace that is untouchable. You then soar to immeasurable heights of success and satisfaction.

Secret #7

Love yourself, love what you do and let others show their love to you.

Love yourself, because you can only give to others what you already possess. Love what you do, and do what you love. And let others show their love to you, whether it comes in the form of a sale or simply a smile.

Quick Summary of Your Sales Flight Plan:

Secret 1

Your thoughts create your reality.

Your thoughts create your beliefs, which create your actions, which create your habits, which create your character.

Sales come to you from sources expected and unexpected.

Secret 2

Compassion creates rapport.

Recognize and react to personality types: Feeling, Information, Big Picture.

Be a co-pilot with your buyers.

Secret 3

Show you care and buyers will share.

Employ the four benefits for gaining the buyer's criteria:

Save them time, make their job easier, make the buyer look good to their boss and make the sales process fun.

Personal passion makes the difference.

Secret 4

See an objection as a buying signal—let go of your fear and the buyer will let go of theirs.

Listen to the buyer with your ears, see their point of view with your eyes and open your heart to what they are feeling.

Ask for all the objections and ask for the business, too.

Don't let your self-esteem be defined by one sale or event.

Secret 5

Focus on your own progress and you will win.

Cooperation can replace competition.

Compete with yourself and expand your comfort zone.

Secret 6

Quiet the thoughts in your mind and you will be comfortable with the silence after asking for the sale.

Closing is a natural result of the sales flight. It is like a plane having a smooth landing.

Remember: ABK—Always Be Kind and ABC-Always Be Connected.

Secret 7

Be a mentor and seek a mentor.

Be a source of solutions and inspiration.

Love yourself, love what you do and let others show their love to you.

Soar to new heights that can't be measured by radar.

Here is one final way to think about how giving of yourself creates success: If you were told that $86,400 would be deposited into your bank account every day and your only responsibility in order to keep the money coming is to spend it all wisely by midnight or it would all be gone, you would gladly do so, right? Well, 86,400 is exactly the number of seconds we are given every day. We have the freedom to choose how to spend our time. Ideally, we spend it wisely—doing our best and making a difference every day. And if we don't, the time is lost to us forever. It's that simple and that important. Whether you are a hard-charging executive or a suburban soccer mom, you may not think you have the time to nurture yourself and others. But if someone told you a secret that would increase your happiness and your success, wouldn't you want to give it a try? I've shared *The 7 Most Powerful Selling Secrets* with you, and making them a part of my daily life has increased my happiness and my success, just as it has for almost everyone I've shared them with. It is my hope that you will try these secrets on for size. I think you'll like the way they fit! (Please visit **www.johnlivesay.com** and sign up for my newsletter so we can stay in touch.)

Bon Voyage!

At the end of Chapter 7 (page 104), you will find a summary of the 7 Secrets. Below are some bonus secrets.

The Most Powerful Bonus Secrets
of Successful Selling

Bonus secrets:

—When you do something for others to enjoy, you get joy

—Look for the excitement of the unexpected moment

—Replace fear with compassion and love

—When you integrate your spirit and your mind, you sell

from your heart and soar!

Ten-Second Meditations /Affirmations

Now that you've seen how powerful your thoughts are in creating your reality, you are empowered to see the results they can have on your happiness, fulfillment and success. The next step is to take action. One way to do that is to use the affirmations suggested throughout the book in your own life. These are among the most important to remember:

Sales come to me from sources expected and unexpected.

I am now a co-pilot with my buyers. My compassion allows them to see me as a trustworthy person.

I relax into the flow of life knowing when to speak and when to listen.

I welcome objections as buying signs with an inner calm and confidence. I listen with an open heart and respond with the right words that give the best results to all concerned.

I am always making progress on the road to success. I stay focused on my own results and growth.

I am comfortable during silence. I am patient.

I share my thoughts, ideas and guidance with all. When I do, I soar to heights that can't be tracked by radar.

Remember that life is a journey—so learn to enjoy the ride! Don't pressure yourself to absorb and remember everything you read the first time through. Often, the best way to implement new ideas is to share them with others. Once you know something well enough to explain it to someone else, you've got it under your belt. You don't have to be perfect to start using or sharing these secrets. Relax into the new you and realize that every great leap is actually made up of many small steps. Take them one at a time, and don't forget to look down and enjoy the view along the way.

Recommended Reading

Love is the Killer App – Tim Sanders

The Influentials – Ed Keller and Jon Berry

Mastering the Complex Sale – Jeff Thull

Roadtrip Nation – Michael Marriner and Nathan Gebhard

The Sales Training Handbook – Jeff Magee

Questions from Earth, Answer from Heaven – Char Margolis

The Sales Athlete – Kathy Aaronson

The One Minute Salesperson – Spencer Johnson

The Four Agreements – Don Miguel Ruiz

A Return to Love – Marianne Williamson

Where Regret Cannot Find Me – David Ault

There is a Spiritual Solution to Every Problem – Dr. Wayne Dyer

Hug Your Customers – Jack Mitchell

The Power of Full Engagement – Jim Loehr and Tony Schwartz

The Spirituality of Success – Vincent Roazzi

Spiritual Marketing – Joe Vitale

Golf for Enlightenment – Deepak Chopra

ORDER FORM   FREE SHIPPING!

To order copies of this book, fill out the form below or call our toll-free number. (This book is available at special quantity discounts for bulk purchases.)

Payable in US funds only. Postage & Handling is free! We accept Visa, MC, checks and money orders. No cash/COD.

Three ways to order:
Call in your order toll-free at 1-866-570-6724
Fax your order form to 1-804-883-5234
Mail your order form to:

Palari Publishing
PO Box 9288
Richmond, VA 23227-0288

☐ Check enclosed ☐ or Bill my credit card_____

Card #_____

Visa or MC?_____

Exp date: month_____/ year_____

CVV2 (last 3 digits on back of card __ __ __)

Signature_____

Name_____

Street_____

City_____

State_____ZIP_____

How many books_____X $19.95 = _____

(VA residents add 4.5% sales tax)   _____

Total amount enclosed   _____

Please allow 2-4 weeks for delivery.

This offer is subject to change without notice.